Praise for
BLENDED LEARNING with Google

"The smart, sassy, southern 'Bell' is at it again! In her new book, Kasey shares incredible insights for how to create dynamic learning experiences in every community, no matter where it is or what it looks like! In these pages, Kasey will help you see new possibilities for the 4Cs. She also shares reflections and calls to action that will help you go beyond the tools to transform both teaching and learning. From pro tips to educator insights to examples of dynamic learning experiences, you will love the ideas that Kasey shares!"

—Ann Kozma, educator innovation lead @Flipgrid

"As a classroom teacher, I think the joy of this book is that it quickly goes from theory to practical, simple classroom examples that can be used to transform teaching right away. Right now with so much learning online, we have to do better. Kasey's book helps all of us do that. Now is the time to pick up this book, discuss it with colleagues, and shake up our blended, distance, hybrid, and face-to-face learning."

—Vicki Davis, @coolcatteacher and host of *10 Minute Teacher Podcast*

"School administrators, if you are looking for a book to enhance teaching, learning, and the intentional use of technology, look no further. *Blended Learning with Google* is a must-have book for your school's professional development! This book is exactly what I have been looking for to share with my staff.

"Kasey Bell is your personal guide to help you and your team learn practical strategies with Google tools to create and support Dynamic Learning. Reflect on your mindset, take a leap, and partner with teacher extraordinaire Kasey Bell to shake up learning in your classroom!"

—Evan Robb, principal, author, and speaker

"Kasey Bell does it again with her new book! It is easy to read, easy to implement and will help educators think differently about how to approach blended learning in the classroom. It is packed full of really useful examples and ways to begin to shift instructional practices. This is sure to be a resource that teachers will go back to over and over again."

—Holly Clark, speaker, blogger, and author of *The Chromebook Infused Classroom*

"Kasey's down-to-earth approach is all about ways teachers can go beyond traditional learning (with some help from Google). This book encourages, supports, and guides educators with practical advice, enlightening anecdotes, and specific actions."

—Tony Vincent, LearninginHand.com

"The art of teaching has never been challenged more than in 2020. Educators around the globe are looking for practical ideas and this book has exactly what we are all looking for. Thanks to Kasey, we can now go beyond our comfort zone and do what is best for all learners."

—Kristin and Joe Merrill, @TheMerrillsEDU, authors of *The InterACTIVE Class series*

KASEY BELL

From the **Shake Up Learning**® Series

BLENDED LEARNING

with Google

Your Guide to **DYNAMIC** Teaching and Learning

Success Strategies for Classroom & Distance Learning in a Post-COVID World

The Bestselling Book by Kasey Bell

Shake Up Learning

*Practical Ideas to Move Learning
from Static to Dynamic*

Over
300 5-Star
Reviews!
★★★★★

"No geek speak here—just fresh ideas, a can-do attitude, and a love for children. That is what we all need to shake up learning, and this is the book and educator to help you do just that!"

—**Vicki Davis,** @coolcatteacher, host of
The 10-Minute Teacher podcast

"This is *the* book for educators wanting to transform their classrooms and schools into dynamic hubs of learning and curiosity. Don't miss your chance to learn from one of the best in this educational page-turner!"

—**Holly Clark,** coauthor of
The Google Infused Classroom

"Kasey's honest approach helps bridge the gap between the big ideas in education and the practical strategies that help teachers create dynamic learning experiences for every student. This is not a book about technology. This is a book about learning!"

—**Alice Keeler,** coauthor of *50 Things You
Can Do with Google Classroom*

"One of the best learning books of all time"

—BookAuthority

"Kasey Bell's fresh perspective on revolutionizing the classroom gives teachers the reasons to push boundaries and take learning to new heights."

—**Tony Vincent,** learning and technology educator,
Tony Vincent, Inc., learninginhand.com

"Kasey Bell puts her finger on the pulse of education in *Shake Up Learning*. The dynamic learning framework she outlines in the book describes the kind of meaningful, authentic learning that students are craving. With discussion questions, a companion website, and room to reflect, this book is packed with resources!"

—**Matt Miller,** speaker, blogger, and
author of *Ditch That Textbook*

Shake Up Learning Online

 Visit **ShakeUpLearning.com** for more information and to subscribe to Kasey's weekly newsletter, loaded with tips, tools, and resources for teachers and educators.

ShakeUpLearning.com

Check out these *free* ebooks from Shake Up Learning!

- Google Classroom Cheat Sheets for Teachers and Students
- The Teacher's Guide to Digital Choice Boards
- The Complete Guide to Google Certifications
- How to Become a Google Certified Trainer
- The Shake Up Learning Quick-Start Guide
- The Top 10 Secrets of an Awesome Tech Coach
- The Guide to Google Drive Sharing

ShakeUpLearning.com/subscribe

Published by Shake Up Learning
Celina, TX
ShakeUpLearning.com

Cover Design by Genesis Kohler
Editing and Interior Design by My Writers' Connection

Library of Congress Control Number: On file
Paperback ISBN: 978-1-7356018-2-3
Ebook ISBN: 978-1-7356018-3-0

For my sister, Wendy Bell, you are my rock and my best friend.

For my niece and nephew, Keaton and Peri Raney, I am so proud of you both. Be bold, be brilliant, and take advantage of everything God's world has to offer. You are capable of more than you know, and I'll always be here to help you reach for the stars.

Contents

Do This First!

As a way of saying thanks for your purchase, I'm offering exclusive access to some amazing resources that make this book interactive.

Visit the Companion Website

Go to **BlendedLearningwithGoogle.com** to explore Kasey's books and free book-related resources.

BlendedLearningwithGoogle.com

Get the Supplement: *Google from A to Z*

There are so many Google tools! It can get confusing. I created a supplement, *Google A to Z: The Google Glossary for Teachers,* so you can easily reference the tools mentioned throughout this book. The supplement also comes in handy as you read other Shake Up Learning books and resources or take one of our online courses.

BlendedLearningwithGoogle.com/atoz

Get the Blended Learning with Google Toolkit!

Consider this your *Blended Learning with Google* cheat sheet. Get this easy reference guide for blended learning strategies aligned with Google tools.

BlendedLearningwithGoogle.com/toolkit

The Blended Learning with Google Workshop
(An Online Companion Course)

As you read this book, you will see references to the companion course that will teach you more specifically how to use the tools and strategies mentioned in this book. The course is completely online, self-paced, and video-based, so you can get hands-on instruction with the author, Google Certified Trainer Kasey Bell.

BlendedLearningwithGoogle.com/course

This course, as well as many other courses from Shake Up Learning, are also available for schools. Go to GoogleTrainingforSchools.com to learn more.

GoogleTrainingforSchools.com

Blended Learning with Google Book Study

 I wrote this book with group book studies in mind. Each chapter includes discussion questions that you can use to facilitate a book study at your school or with your organization. We also offer online book studies throughout the year, as well as book study packages including bulk discounts on books, swag, and access to images and questions to make the most of your book study.

BlendedLearningwithGoogle.com/bookstudy

Join the Community

 Go to ShakeUpLearning.com/community to join our free Facebook community and connect with like-minded educators.

ShakeUpLearning.com/community

Which Book Should I Read First?

This is the second book in the *Shake Up Learning* series. While the first book isn't a prerequisite, it is recommended as it goes deeper into the foundational principles of Dynamic Learning. *Blended Learning with Google* will review the framework but focuses more on the application of Dynamic Learning with Google tools.

Introduction

What's shakin' y'all? Bless your heart for picking up this book! If you don't know me, my name is Kasey. I am a sassy southern "Bell!" Literally, my last name is Bell, and I'm known for saying all kinds of quirky southern things like *y'all*. I hail from a little town in Northeast Texas—Paris, Texas. We have our very own Eiffel Tower, complete with a red cowboy hat on top. Football and sweet tea are in my veins, and I might call you *sugar*, *sweetie*, or *honey* from time to time. My Texas roots run deep, and so does my love for teaching, learning, and doing what's best for students. The good Lord gave me a heart for kids and a big teacher voice. Throughout this book, you may find some southern sayings, quotes, and quirks. And if you don't get it at first, well, bless your heart! Keep reading; I'm sure you'll catch on soon enough!

I do my very best to stay positive, especially in public, but it's hard not to get frustrated with the state of education. I may look calm and collected on the outside, but inside I'm throwing a hissy fit. *We can do so much better!* Education is in desperate need of a shakeup, thus my motto, my books, and my blood, sweat, and tears.

There are many great ideas for the classroom—great books, great research, and great resources, but I'm a practical woman, so this book is all about action! You may know people who talk a good talk but are all hat and no cattle (which in Texas means you are all talk and no action). Well, this book is all about *action*, my friend! And I'm gonna two-step you all the way. Go big or go home, y'all!

Was that too much Texan for ya? Don't worry, I'll be translating Texan to English for you throughout this book. I promise to keep it to a minimum. But just in case you are new to the southern vernacular, let's start with the guide to *y'all*:

Now, don't you worry! We are in this together. Consider me your Google tour guide. I'm going to stay focused on practical ideas and strategies to take your classroom to the next level. You will learn about Google tools, meaningful strategies to make your lessons more dynamic, and some of my favorite tips and tricks along the way.

As I am putting the final touches on this book, I am sitting outside a hospital, wearing a face mask, and praying my loved ones are safe and healthy. COVID-19 has left its mark on the world. Education as we know it has forever been changed. For how long and to what degree has yet to be determined, but already teachers, many of whom may have previously resisted technology, suddenly find themselves thrown headfirst into the online learning space. Sink or swim, teachers are showing up every day for their students virtually, creating new learning experiences for their students, and trying new things. Those who have been afraid to get out of their comfort zones have now come to expect their jobs to be uncomfortable.

In this book, you will read about missed opportunities. Well, the Coronavirus has presented education with crisis, but it also offers a huge opportunity that you *definitely* don't want to miss. The Dynamic Learning Framework I use in this book and explain more fully in *Shake Up Learning* has a whole new relevance in the wake of emergency school closures and remote learning. Taking risks, failing forward, and doing what's best for kids has always been what the Shake Up Learning philosophy is about. My hope is that, with this opportunity, we are brave enough to make big changes in the education system and in our classrooms—and that more educators and educational leaders will place greater importance on preparing students for this technology-driven world.

ABOUT THIS BOOK

When I wrote *Shake Up Learning: Practical Ideas to Move Learning from Static to Dynamic*, I didn't know whether anybody would actually read it or understand the framework that I was presenting. But after the success of the book, and with the transformation I have seen in so many classrooms, I decided to write a follow-up to explain how to easily use Google tools to make learning dynamic.

My first book outlines the foundation of the Dynamic Learning Model and Framework, which we will use throughout this book. The first book is recommended reading, but not required. If you're familiar with *Shake Up Learning,* you may notice that a few of the lessons from that book are repeated here. I did this for several reasons: First of all, it's a good review. Second, I wanted to go a little bit deeper in discussing the application of Google tools to these lessons. And finally, I wanted to be sure that if anyone skips book one, you still get these high-quality, high-yield strategies for your classroom.

In this follow-up, we are going to go deeper into Dynamic Blended Learning and explore ways to support these ideas with Google tools. **That said, this is *not* a book about Google. This is a book about *learning*!** Technology is *not* a magic solution for our problems in education. Technology simply and powerfully presents an opportunity to do things differently and to create Dynamic Learning experiences for our students.

That same truth applies to Google tools: Google isn't a magic solution. Don't get me wrong; I love Google tools and use them in pretty much everything I do and create. But Google is not what matters. What matters is that we take the opportunity to use every tool at our disposal to increase learning and engagement. Student learning and doing what's best for kids is the bottom line.

This book is the culmination of the work that I've been doing for many years now. Even as I'm writing this, I'm discovering so many things that I have done, created, or presented on the idea of blended learning and blended learning with Google. But my hope is to bring together the knowledge, the experience, the tips, the tricks— all-encompassing best practices in blended learning to help you become the best twenty-first-century teacher you can be.

Given the timing of the release of this book, it could have been titled, *Remote Learning with Google, Home Learning with Google,* or even *OMGoogle! Help me, Kasey!* But I'm striving to share strategies that will carry us far beyond this defining moment. If you focus on the strategy and not the tool, you will be able to adapt and grow as the technology (and the world) changes.

Who should read this book?

Blended Learning with Google is for K–12 classroom teachers, educators, school leaders, and anyone who wants to improve teaching and learning. I'm sure you've been disappointed in the past when you've heard about an idea that sounds great but just isn't practical because of the time or expense it requires to implement. You won't find those ideas in this book. I am a fan of keeping things practical, so I will be breaking lessons and tools down into meaningful steps that any teacher can follow. This book is for all educators, from the tech newbie to the tech expert. I got you covered!

Will this book help me with distance teaching and learning?

Yes! Many of the ideas in this book can be used in distance learning. This book will show you new ways to use the Google tools you know and love, and it may introduce you to new tools you never knew existed, especially if you keep the supplemental *Google A to Z Glossary* handy. I will also be sharing my best distance (aka remote or online) learning tips along the way.

Do I have to be a Google expert?

No! This book is focused on implementation and pedagogy, not the tool. You will, however, gain an awareness of the capabilities of Google tools and expand your digital toolbox.

What I really want you to see is how you can use technology tools to create Dynamic Learning experiences in your classroom. So even if your school hasn't adopted Google for Education, you can implement ideas from this book, using whatever tools you have available. Again, this book isn't about Google; it is about helping teachers go *beyond* traditional, static learning.

If you are brand new to Google, you may want or need additional support. I highly recommend you grab a copy of the supplemental *Google A to Z Glossary* to help you get a better understanding of Google tools. And if you need some hands-on tutorials, join the "Blended Learning with Google" online workshop.

How to Interact with This Book

I've created a companion website, BlendedLearningwithGoogle.com, to make this experience more dynamic for you, the reader. If you follow Shake Up Learning, you know that I love resources, and I have put together a website loaded with additional resources, including any new goodies I discover after the publishing of this book. On the site, you will find a dedicated page for each chapter, plus resources, downloads, templates, and a searchable lesson plan database for YOU!

Each chapter contains questions to ponder on your own or use for your own book study with your colleagues. At the end of each chapter you will find the following:

- **Link to Chapter Resources**—Each chapter has a dedicated page on BlendedLearningwithGoogle.com where you can find resources mentioned in the chapter, as well as supplemental resources to help you extend the learning.

- **Discussion and Reflection Questions**—These questions are designed to help you think critically about the chapter and how it applies to you. You may use these as reflection questions to answer independently or to discuss with your colleagues or book study group. You can also take it a step further and share your answers online in the Shake Up Learning community on Facebook (shakeuplearning.com/community), or on your favorite social media platform, using the #shakeuplearning hashtag.

- **Reflection Space**—I've included some blank real estate in this book to give you room to write, sketch, draw, doodle, whatever you need. I encourage you to take advantage of this process to help digest the book and the process and to reflect on any actions you have taken.

Watch for These Icons!

Chapter Resources

At the end of each chapter, you will find a unique link and QR code that will take you to a dedicated page of links and resources for that chapter.

Missed Opportunities

Nothing gets my goat more than a missed opportunity! Sometimes we miss opportunities because we don't know what to look for. Watch for the Missed Opportunities icon to heighten your awareness of new tools and ideas to shake up learning in your classroom.

Remote Learning Tips

COVID-19 has ushered in a new age of remote teaching and learning. I'll be sharing specific remote learning tips and best practices along the way.

Pro Tips

Watch for the Pro Tips icon. These Google tips will save you time and frustration and empower you to level-up your use of technology in the classroom.

Google from A to Z Supplement References

Don't forget to use the supplement to help you better understand the tools as you progress through this book. Keep it handy to reference any unfamiliar Google tools.

What You *Won't* Find in This Book

This book is not a how-to-use Google book with technical, step-by-step tutorials. If it were, it would be out of date as soon as it was published.

But if you need that, I got your back! The companion course, The Blended Learning with Google Workshop, aligns with every chapter in this book to show you exactly how you and your students can create these in Google tools. What you will find are practical strategies for using Google tools to support Dynamic Learning in your classroom.

What about Updates?— Prepare Yourself!

Speaking of out-of-date references, Google changes ALL THE TIME. This is a good thing, but it makes it difficult to keep everything up to date in this book. While the book is focused on strategy and not the "how-to" side of Google, some screenshots may look out of date, vocabulary is bound to change (Google loves to change names), and menus and features are expected to change. One of the best skills we can learn as teachers, and pass on to our students, is the ability to teach ourselves new skills, especially when it comes to technology. If something looks or sounds different, adapt; click around on your own, and you can figure it out. I can't spoon feed you technology. I've even had to figure out Google updates on the fly in the middle of hosting a training session or workshop. But as Marie Forleo says in her book by the same title, "Everything is *figureoutable*." This part is up to you, so prepare yourself for the exciting and ever-changing world of Google.

Guess what I do when I don't know how to use the updated features in Google tools? I do exactly what you do; I "Google it!"

A Note about COPPA and CIPA

Before we dive in, it's important to mention that COPPA and CIPA, as well as other governing laws in your state and country, may affect who can access. Some of the apps listed are restricted to those who are thirteen years old or older. Because this requirement changes as apps are updated, please comply with all of the laws and policies when using any digital tools with your students.

Beyond Blended Learning

Before we begin, please pause to check in on your mindset.

- Are you willing to try new things in your lesson planning?
- Are you open to exploring different ways to use technology to engage students?
- Are you willing to try again if things don't go exactly right the first time?

I sure hope your answer to each of those questions is *yes*! How many times have you accepted defeat before even trying? We are so quick to limit ourselves, deciding who we are and aren't. Here's the deal: None of the amazing learning opportunities, tools, or strategies we're about to explore together will matter in *your* classroom or online setting if you aren't ready to consider and try new ideas. If you are truly going to shake up learning for your students, you need a growth mindset. That means being open to a shift in traditional education and pushing the normal bounds of school.

So are you ready to say goodbye to boring lectures, sit and get, and the same old, tired projects? Are you ready to move the learning in your classroom from static, one-and-done activities, to more dynamic learning?

Good! Me too! Let's shake things up!

Chapter 1

Shaking Up the Game of School

When it comes to talking about our broken school system, I tend to end up a little feisty and standing tall on my soapbox! As we say in the south, "That really gets my goat!" And yes, I've said that during a keynote on stage in front of thousands. I am passionate about making meaningful changes in education, and the changes start with us, the teachers.

For many students and teachers, school has become a game of compliance and test scores. Listening to lectures, taking notes, putting your name on your paper, staying in your seat, and turning in work on time have been mainstays for success. High achievers master this game by the time they reach the middle grades, but where is the evidence of their learning?

Why are grades so focused on behaviors instead of learning? Are we creating an army of test-takers or creative thinkers? Are we training people to perform like robots, or do we want to produce unique and innovative *humans* who can contribute meaningfully to society?

Even as COVID-19 has shaken the education system, I still see a focus on seat time, as teachers are encouraged to try to replicate the school day online. Seat time does not equal learning! We have to use this opportunity to pivot and improve, not keep trying to fit a square peg in a round hole. If we're really going to prepare students for their future, we have to disrupt the game of school and shift the education model from static to dynamic.

RETHINK DIGITAL ASSIGNMENTS

If you want to transition your classroom to an online or blended environment, you must rethink traditional assignments and how you use technology. Just because you make your lesson or assignment digital doesn't mean that it will work the same way it did on paper or face-to-face. We have to rethink digital assignments! A digital worksheet is still a worksheet, and sometimes digitizing analog assignments actually makes them more confusing and time-consuming. Enter Dynamic Learning! Dynamic Learning is all about going **beyond** traditional assignments and traditional learning, even **beyond** what was previously possible.

What Is Blended Learning?

There are many different ways to define blended learning and several blended learning models. And as the technology and the world's challenges and opportunities continue to shape the way we learn, these models continue to evolve and grow. As the lines continue to blur with what can be delivered online, the idea of blended learning can take many forms. Now that so many schools have been forced to get creative with delivering learning from afar, you may have also heard the terms *synchronous* and *asynchronous* learning.

If you look up the definition of blended learning, meaning you Google it, you will find a host of different opinions, definitions, and perspectives on what blended learning is or should be. Combine that with the unbelievable changes and challenges of a worldwide pandemic, and you've a smorgasbord of new buzzwords, definitions, and models.

Here's how I define blended learning:

Blended learning is the combination of face-to-face instruction and online learning. This definition encompasses the concepts and ideas I have been teaching for many years. In fact, pretty much every blog post on ShakeUpLearning.com can be categorized as blended learning. Clean and simple, but it leaves a lot on the table. That's why I created a blended learning framework that would incorporate best practices and push the boundaries of traditional teaching practices.

Enter Dynamic Learning. My definition of dynamic learning is continuing to evolve and grow, as best practices should. You'll see that the definition below has been revised since the first *Shake Up Learning* book.

Dynamic Blended Learning:

Dynamic blended learning is characterized by constant change and activity, growing and evolving over time. This learning can take place anywhere, anytime, and it is personalized and differentiated. It is learner-centered, giving students choice and embedding communication, collaboration, critical thinking, and creativity skills where they align with the learning goals. Dynamic blended learning also extends beyond the traditional bounds of the school day, schedule, and physical walls, and beyond the physical notion of hard and fast due dates. Digital tools are used for more than substitution, to do and create previously unconceived things. Dynamic learning is boundless, with limitless opportunities.

Dynamic Learning...

- Is learnER-centered
- Is learnING-centered
- Is focused on learning targets
- Includes one or more of the four Cs
- Goes beyond traditional limitations

Dynamic Learning IS NOT...

- Just using technology in the classroom
- Digitizing assignments
- Substituting tech for paper
- Replicating the traditional school day in an online environment

What Is Static Learning?

To help you better understand the idea of Dynamic Learning, let's begin with something you are most likely familiar with: Static Learning. *Static learning* is the old-school way of teaching. It's the way I was taught and the way I taught in my classroom for the first few years. (You don't know what you don't know! As Maya Angelou taught us, "Do the best you can until you know better. Then when you know better, do better!")

Static learning is learning that lacks movement, action, or change. With this unengaging model of education, learning happens in short bursts and is often demonstrated through one-and-done activities, short-term assignments, or worksheets (even digital worksheets), which are confined within the traditional bounds of the school system, school day, and school walls.

Why do we put so many limitations on learning? Our students deserve so much more than static one-and-done!

Take a look on social media, and you'll find thousands of amazing education ideas and trends; dynamic learning is a way to blend the ideas that are best for *your* students into lessons and activities that are meaningful and valuable. The goal isn't to do *everything*. Rather, it is to use diverse activities to make learning engaging and to empower students to develop and apply newly acquired skills in practical ways. We can do that when we use The Dynamic Learning Model. Think of dynamic learning as blended learning on steroids!

As you begin to adapt to the evolution of technology and evolution of education, you may also encounter some new terminology. Let's clarify, for the purpose of creating meaning, *blended* and *dynamic* learning experiences for students.

In general, the terms *synchronous learning* and *asynchronous learning* have historically referred to *online learning*. As the lines between online, distance, remote, and blended learning get blurred, these definitions will continue to grow and evolve.

Synchronous online activities are those that require students and instructors to be online at the same time. Instructions, lessons, discussions, and presentations occur at a specific time. All students must be online at that specific time to participate (*not flexible*).

Synchronous Examples:

- Zoom/Google Meet live classes; for example, every student must join a Zoom call at 9:00 for a live lesson.
- Students collaborating in a Google Doc/Slide at the same time
- Assigned work time during a live meeting (even if they turn their camera off); for example, Work on X assignment from 11:00–11:30.

Asynchronous online activities are just the opposite. Instructions, lessons, discussions, and presentations occur at different times for each student. Teachers provide materials, instructions, lessons, and assignments that can be accessed over an extended period. Students are given a timeframe or due dates to complete the work and watch lessons and videos. Interactions and discussions take place using asynchronous tools such as discussion boards that do not require everyone to be connected at the same time (*flexible*).

Asynchronous activities require some student autonomy and ability to self-direct, as well as monitoring of progress.

Asynchronous Examples:

- Zoom or Google Meet video recordings where the lesson video is posted online, and students can watch at different times.
- Students are contributing to a collaborative Google Doc/Slide at different times.
- For example, give a week's worth of assignments at the beginning of the week, and students take ownership to complete assignments within the timeframe (*flexible work time*).

Blended learning is a combination of face-to-face and online learning, so it combines any number of these strategies.

Every student doesn't have to do the exact same thing at the exact same time. This was a tough lesson for me to learn as a teacher. The more we integrate student choice and asynchronous activities for our students, the more we can differentiate and personalize for our students and meet the demands of ever-changing schedules.

Most of the learning experiences shared in this book can be facilitated in a synchronous or asynchronous environment, because Google tools can be used at the same time or different times. Although I wanted to create a follow-up to my first book, using my own Dynamic Learning Framework, I also wanted to make it clear where this model fits in the spectrum of various learning models. Most of what I teach, create, and share on ShakeUpLearning.com falls under the umbrella of blended learning. Some things are best facilitated in person; others are well suited for online environments. What makes Dynamic Learning different are the key characteristics that take it from just blended to **dynamic** blended learning. Go BEYOND Blended, make it DYNAMIC!

THE DYNAMIC LEARNING MODEL

Take a look at Figure 1.

At the center of it all (the target, if you will) is the goal: Dynamic Learning—not technology, and definitely not Google!

The first circle around Dynamic Learning contains the four Cs: creativity, communication, collaboration, and critical thinking. These elements are foundational for creating meaningful blended learning experiences for students.

Moving outward, the icons in the next circle represent the ways we can go beyond traditional learning to create Dynamic Learning. (We will talk more about the "Beyonds" in the next chapter.)

- Beyond the Bell
- Beyond the Grade Level and Subject Area
- Beyond the Walls
- Beyond the Tools
- Beyond the Due Date

The outer ring is all about planning and implementation, represented as a cycle, similar to the learning cycle itself:

- Purposeful Planning
- Focused on Learning Outcomes
- Fearless Implementation
- Facilitated with Finesse
- Honest Reflection
- Share with the World

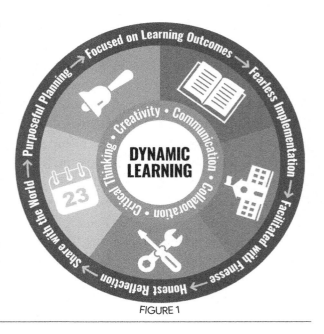

FIGURE 1

Note that the word *technology* isn't explicitly present in any part of the Dynamic Learning Model. That's because technology is rarely the focus or end goal. Technology is a part of everything we do. With intention we can infuse technology in the classroom to enhance learning.

Essential Components for Dynamic Learning

Dynamic Learning is not a task that can simply be checked off a list. Just like teaching, it is more art than science. Even with small tweaks, you will begin to see tiny transformations in your classroom. If you are ready for a bigger leap and want the learning to truly become more dynamic, begin by incorporating (or increasing the use of) these essential components.

The Four Cs

At the heart of the Dynamic Learning Model are the four Cs: creativity, communication, collaboration, and critical thinking skills. Foundational for learning transformation, the four Cs help prepare students for the future. Every time I walk into a classroom and see something amazing, at least one of the four Cs are present, if not more. Every Dynamic Learning experience should include at least one of the four Cs.

For our purposes, we will define these skills as the following:

Creativity: The use of imagination and original ideas to solve problems and create (Examples: Cultivate creativity and innovation with projects that require students to design original solutions, invent something new to solve a problem, or integrate art and design, with room to fail.)

Communication: The ability to effectively and clearly communicate for a variety of audiences and using a variety of tools and mediums (Examples: Give students opportunities to interact with adult experts, authors, and real-world audiences. Let them experience speaking and presenting.)

Collaboration: Learning and working in groups or teams, locally or globally, to achieve a goal (Examples: Ensure that there is purpose to the collaboration and not just group work. Form partners and teams strategically, with assigned leadership roles, include team-building exercises, and establish collaboration guidelines and shared decision-making.)

Critical Thinking: The ability to conceptualize, analyze, synthesize, and evaluate information for the purpose of deeper understanding, problem-solving, and guiding action (Examples: Create learning experiences, such as mock trials or debates, scientific investigations, interpreting events in history or literature, or design challenges.)

In what ways are you already integrating the four Cs into your curriculum? Notice again that each of these is not explicitly talking about using technology. It's about active learning and skills for the twenty-first century. Every Dynamic Learning experience should integrate one or more of the four Cs with a purpose of working toward the learning targets. They also work together very seamlessly, and all can be implemented across grade levels and subject areas.

CHANGE YOUR VOCABULARY

If we are to ever truly move beyond technology as a substitution, we must get rid of terms that are rooted in old-school, paper-based assignments. Words such as *paperless, notebook, packet, worksheet, poster, cards,* etc., can limit our perception of what's possible.

Terms like *interactive notebook,* for example, may sound techy, but the connotation of taking the paper-based notebook and images and putting them online in a presentation software limits the possibilities.

What if instead of talking about *notebooks,* a word that soon will have little meaning for future-ready students, we start using terms such as *learning streams* to describe the various ways students can create, collaborate, and share content for audiences far beyond the school walls. Heck, if we can call things *snaps* and *tiktoks,* you can even give new ideas new names, such as "ram-a-lam-a-ding-dong," or call something a "thing-a-ma-jig," if you like.

As you update and redefine your teaching methods, consider what new and creative words and phrases better describe the kind of learning you want to see happening in your classroom.

The ISTE Standards for Students

I also believe that the ISTE Standards for Students are an important foundation for meaningful digital learning. They intertwine with the four Cs and are learner-driven and student-centered. These standards give us a foundation for building critical, Dynamic Learning experiences.

Although these standards are not explicitly part of the Dynamic Learning Model, they align nicely to the four Cs and the "Beyonds" by pushing learning to a higher level and expanding ways we can go beyond old-school assignments.

If you are not familiar with the ISTE Standards for Students, you can take a deeper look at each standard on the ISTE website: shakeup.link/istes.

Your Own Content and Grade-Level Standards

Your content-area and grade-level standards are the most important in *your* planning and teaching. Use these standards to drive the creation of specific learning goals, development of assessments, and creation of meaningful, dynamic learning experiences for your students.

What Does Google Have to Do with Dynamic Learning?

I mentioned earlier that technology can enhance learning when we use it intentionally. I've always believed that technology, including the Google tools you'll learn about in this book, presents us with an opportunity to create more dynamic learning experiences for our students.

These days, "going Google" is a no-brainer. Google for Education is free, readily accessible from any device 24/7, and offers a suite of tools that support teaching and learning. I don't work for Google. Google didn't pay me any money to write this book. I support what I believe in, and I've seen firsthand how Google tools can be used to implement the strategies that transform learning from boring and stagnant to dynamic.

The strategies in this book are meant to be adapted for your classroom, so you can call this a custom blend. There are specific lesson plans in which you can see exactly which dynamic learning characteristics have been applied, as well as which of the four Cs and ISTE standards. As you look at these strategies, choosing among them will depend on you, the teacher, and what characteristics you choose to use in your own lesson plans.

Remember: Technology is *not* a magic solution for education. It does, however, provide an opportunity to do things differently, to deepen the learning, to engage students in new ways. Put simply, technology tools such as Google provide an opportunity for Dynamic Blended Learning.

Online Resources for Chapter 1

Here you will find resources mentioned in Chapter 1, supplemental resources, videos, as well as new and updated resources.

BlendedLearningwithGoogle.com/1

Online Course: Module 1

Dig deeper and get hands-on tutorials in the online course. This chapter aligns with Module 1 in the course.

BlendedLearningwithGoogle.com/course

Discussion Questions

- How would you describe your classroom? Are the learning experiences static or dynamic?
- Think about the idea of synchronous vs asynchronous online learning. How can you find a balance between these two in your classroom?
- How often do you integrate the four Cs in your lessons? Why?

Notes & Reflection Space

Beyond Blended Learning (The Five Bs)

The Dynamic Learning Model is at the center of what I refer to as the Dynamic Learning Framework, which focuses on five Dynamic Learning Characteristics. These characteristics make it possible to go beyond static, one-and-done activities. In this chapter, we will take a closer look at the framework (Figure 2) and break down each characteristic. I refer to the five Dynamic Learning Characteristics in the framework as the "Beyonds." You can call them the five Bs for short.

Characteristic #1: Beyond the Bell

Learning doesn't have to end when the bell rings, or whatever signals the end of the school day. With digital tools and devices that are available twenty-four hours a day and seven days a week, students can continue to learn, collaborate, grow, and dig deeper into their learning on their own terms. Please note: When I talk about extending learning beyond the school day, I don't mean homework. Going beyond the bell means developing the mindset that learning can take place anytime and anywhere. To become dynamic learners, students must learn how to take ownership of not only their learning but also their time. As teachers, we must help student move

beyond the game of school. We want students to understand that they have the power to connect and learn, and to teach themselves new concepts and skills.

Characteristic #2: Beyond the Grade Level and Subject Area

The education system we have today is still based on a factory model in which students are basically placed on a factory conveyor belt. What they learn is what fits inside the factory "box," all dictated by their ages and grade levels. We have to think of learning as something much more flexible. We've now seen firsthand how flexible teachers and students must be with distance and remote learning. What we're seeing and experiencing in a post-COVID world is that this factory model of learning doesn't work well for today's culture—and is especially ineffective for personalized and distance learning. Let this challenge guide us to make meaningful changes in education. Let's take kids off the conveyor belt of education, give them opportunities to explore the world and move beyond the subject areas we teach, and find their interests and passions. Learning doesn't have to fit inside a box or the traditional ideas of a school system designed long ago.

FIGURE 2

DYNAMIC LEARNING

Use these strategies to go BEYOND traditional learning and make it more DYNAMIC!

BEYOND THE BELL

Learning doesn't have to end when the bell rings. With digital tools and devices that are available 24/7, students can continue to learn, collaborate, grow, and dig deeper into their learning on their own terms. This doesn't mean homework. This is a mindset for students that means learning can take place anytime, anywhere, and students can own it.

BEYOND THE GRADE LEVEL & SUBJECT

Let's take kids off the conveyor belt of education and give them opportunities to learn about the things that interest them beyond the subject areas we teach and even beyond what it says they should learn in each grade level. Learning doesn't have to fit inside a box.

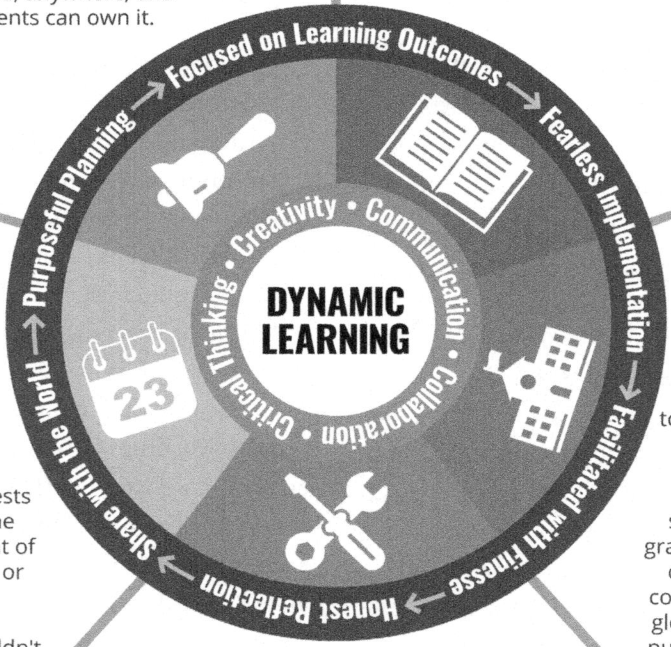

Focused on Learning Outcomes → Fearless Implementation → Facilitated with Finesse → Honest Reflection → Share with the World → Purposeful Planning →

Creativity • Communication • Collaboration • Critical Thinking

DYNAMIC LEARNING

BEYOND THE DUE DATE

Consider allowing students to continue the work that interests them beyond the final assessment of the assignment or task. Thinking, learning, and exploring, shouldn't be stifled simply because it was time to turn it in.

BEYOND THE WALLS

Bring the world to your students, and bring your students to the world! Every student in every grade should have opportunities to connect and learn globally as well as publish their work for a global and intentional audience.

BEYOND THE TOOLS

Think beyond using digital tools to do traditional things like typing a paper. Use digital tools to do NEW things! Just going paperless or digital isn't enough; use tools to go further, go deeper and extend the learning, and consider using tools in alternative ways—beyond their original purpose.

shakeup.link/dynamic

Characteristic #3: Beyond the Walls

Going beyond the walls is two-sided, both bringing the outside world into our classrooms and connecting and sharing our classroom and student work with the outside world. Goodness gracious, how this characteristic rings more true now than ever! Remote learning has become essential, and breaking down walls went from "nice to have" to "need to have." Every student in every grade should have opportunities to connect and learn globally. Do you allow your students to publish their work for a global audience? Are you bringing the outside world into your classroom through global collaboration, virtual field trips, video chats, and more? I've asked these questions to countless audiences across the country, and what I've come to realize is that many educators don't realize how easy it can be to connect their classrooms to global resources. The possibilities are endless! To prepare students for our increasingly connected world, we must make global connections a priority and give students the skills need to survive.

Characteristic #4: Beyond the Tools

Think beyond using digital tools to complete traditional assignments, such as papers and reports. If we are going to go Beyond the Tools, going paperless or digital isn't enough. Replicating our face-to face activities in an online environment is easier said than done. We have to rethink how we use technology and move beyond simple substitution. We must use digital tools for new kinds of teaching and to promote deeper learning. Reach beyond what you think a digital tool can do and should be used for. Challenge your students to demonstrate their learning in new ways.

Characteristic #5: Beyond the Due Date

Remember that flexibility that I mentioned earlier? Let's do another backbend and stretch our mindset even further. Consider allowing students to continue work that interests them beyond the final assessment of an assignment or task. Thinking, learning, and exploring shouldn't be stifled simply because the submission deadline arrives.

This characteristic might be the one that teachers struggle with the most. This isn't about giving students extra time to complete an assignment. This is about capitalizing on the learning sparks we see in our students, coaching and mentoring them to find their interests and passions. Moving toward more Dynamic Learning Experiences means moving away from the one-and-done mentality, creating more experiences that live, grow, and evolve over time. Many workplace projects are not one-and-done tasks. Often the work environment is cyclical, like the school year, where we get to improve, try new things, and make revisions each year. Real-world learning never ends.

Dynamic Learning pushes the boundaries of education, going *beyond* the idea of the traditional school day, beyond the physical location of the classroom, beyond using tools as digital substitutes, or even beyond the traditional notion of hard-and-fast due dates. Everything we thought we knew about school and how the school day should work was ripped into pieces when schools shut down during the pandemic. We had to get creative! Learning can and should look different.

When you think about using technology for dynamic teaching and learning, I want you to remember these five characteristics. Use technology to go *beyond* what was previously possible.

Our goal is to use technology tools to create dynamic, blended learning experiences that can't be replicated with pencil and paper.

That's what the rest of this book is about. So let's dive in!

Online Resources for Chapter 2

Here you will find resources mentioned in Chapter 2, supplemental resources, videos, as well as new and updated resources.

**BlendedLearningwithGoogle.com/2**

Online Course: Module 2

Dig deeper and get hands-on tutorials in the online course. This chapter aligns with Module 2 in the course.

BlendedLearningwithGoogle.com/course

Discussion Questions

- Review the Dynamic Learning Framework and characteristics (the five Bs). Which of the five Bs have you already tried in your classroom? Which ones do you want to try?
- How do you help students build a growth mindset? (Beyond the Bell)
- What boundaries in your classroom, or in education in general, do you want to push?

Notes & Reflection Space

_____

_____

_____

_____

_____

_____

_____

_____

_____

_____

_____

_____

_____

_____

_____

Dynamic Blended Learning with Google Tools

So how does Google come into play with the Dynamic Learning Framework, and all the components and characteristics we just covered? Well, Google for Education offers educators and students many tools that support the principles of Dynamic Learning. Remember, Dynamic Learning is not about Google, and it certainly isn't about getting distracted by shiny, techy tools. The purpose of using technology in any form in the classroom is to support Dynamic, Blended Learning. Digital tools, such as Google for Education, present us with a unique opportunity to do things differently, to engage students in new ways, and to inspire them to explore and create!

The truth is, there is no shortage of tools and resources available to help us learn and improve as teachers. (Resources are my jam! You will find a ton of additional resources at shakeuplearning. com to help make Dynamic Learning a reality in your classroom.) But let me be clear: Google tools aren't inherently dynamic. Just because you are using technology doesn't mean an activity is dynamic. It's what you do with these tools to engage students with content and to empower them to teach themselves new skills, and how you use them tap into the four Cs that can make or break a lesson.

Let's take a closer look at the Dynamic Learning Characteristics and strategies for your classroom. I am going to show you how you can use Google tools to support Dynamic Learning experiences for your students.

To avoid the risk of allowing tools to drive, rather than support, learning, we will approach each Dynamic Learning Characteristic (the *Beyonds*) by activity or learning intention. Please keep in mind that even though we are discussing each Dynamic Learning Characteristic separately, they do not have to exist in a silo. You can include as many characteristics as you would like, so long as they help your students reach their learning goals. Although the chapters are organized by characteristic, there will be overlap of characteristics in these strategies. Many strategies will help you integrate more than one of the five Bs.

BEYOND GOOGLE

You'll find many lesson plans in my first book, *Shake Up Learning*, as well as in my online database of shared lesson plans. Most of these lesson plans involve some sort of Google tool, but remember that you aren't limited to Google. The skills and approaches I teach transfer to many other tools. Choose what works for you and your students.

DO THIS, NOT THAT

To illustrate the difference between static and dynamic learning, I have put together a "Do This, Not That" list of learning experiences. As we begin to dig deeper, I want to be clear: Dynamic Learning does not hinge on technology or digital tools. In fact, the word *technology* is not included in the Dynamic Learning definition or in the framework's description. That's because technology can be integrated anywhere. Technology should be seamlessly infused into lessons in such a way that it enhances learning. Dynamic Learning might include this use of digital tools, or it might not. Technology is not a requirement for Dynamic Learning, but it can make Dynamic Learning possible.

Do This	Not That	Grade
Students create an interactive timeline with Google Slides, including images, links, and even video.	Fill-in-the-blank timeline worksheet	3–12
Students tell a story through comic strips in Google Slides or Google Drawings.	Traditional presentation about an important event in history, like the Battle of Waterloo	4–12
Students tell a personal story with Google Slides, including illustrations and narration.	Personal narrative essay	5–12
Students create and solve their own word problem and illustrate it as a story, using Jamboard or Google Drawings.	Solving a word problem from the textbook	3–12
Students conduct an environmental study, surveying the community with Google Forms, analyzing data with Google Sheets.	Research paper about environmental impact	6–12
Students create models and equations in an interactive Google Sheet.	Making 5, 10, or 15 with manipulatives	K–2
Students track their reading over time in a Google Sheets reading tracker.	Paper reading logs	3–12
Students write a story and create an ebook in Google Slides for younger children to teach a concept.	Explaining a concept in a traditional presentation	5–12
Students conduct a Google Meet interview with a war survivor in another country.	Traditional research "paper" on an important war in history	6–12
Students create a collaborative and interactive eBook in Google Slides about the life of Edgar Allan Poe (or other notable) and published for a global audience.	Edgar Allan Poe author study worksheet packet	6–12
Students create a collaborative Google Earth tour project, touring the capitals of the United States, including images, links, and videos, then sharing with other classes.	Labeling and coloring a paper map of the capitals of the United States	4–12
Students create a collaborative public class website in Google Sites on inspiring historical figures (past and present), in which additional content is added throughout the year.	Written biography of Winston Churchill	6–12
Students create an interactive website and blog in Google Sites about their project, including hypothesis, data, video of experiments, reflections, milestones, conclusion, and a place for comments.	Tri-fold poster display of a science fair project	6–12
Students design a new product prototype in Google Drawings that solves a real-world problem.	Worksheet about conflict and resolution	6–12

Chapter 3

Beyond the Bell

The school bell, which has signaled so many beginnings and endings—the start and end of the school day—doesn't have to define the start and end to learning. I remember how my middle school students so obviously anticipated the ring of the final bell each day. They reminded me of Fred Flintstone at the end of the workday, excited to be done and slide down the tail of a dinosaur. Your students may show the same enthusiasm for leaving school, and in some respects, that makes sense: Students and teachers often refer to assignments and activities as *work*. The bell signifies the end of their workday—and the start of something fun.

But what if they believed learning could be fun and self-initiated? As we begin this chapter, I want to set the expectation: Going "Beyond the Bell" is about creating a mindset, *not* about assigning work after the school bell rings. This isn't about homework! The goal of Beyond the Bell activities is to help students recognize learning, know how to seek out their own learning, and develop a growth mindset—building lifelong learners.

We cannot replicate the school day online. We have to break the traditional school day mindset—that school has to look a certain way. That is a mindset. Let it go. It's time to rethink school and innovate.

Our mission is to move away from one-and-done work and to help our students explore learning opportunities everywhere, even outside of school. I want them to understand that, when they are on the bus home searching YouTube for a Minecraft trick, *that* is learning. I want them to realize that learning is something they can own; it doesn't belong to the teacher or the school.

During quarantine and emergency school closures, students have experienced a critical shift that can aid in building this mindset. Learning has taken place outside of the school walls. However, depending on implementation, the student may feel that the teacher must be present to learn. We want students to embrace the idea that learning is something they own, not the teacher.

Learning is something that can take place anytime, anywhere. When students understand that, they will leave our doors equipped with a mindset that enables them to tackle the challenges of the twenty-first century—a century that requires us to accept advancements, embrace changes, and become lifelong, adaptable learners. What follows are a few ways Google tools can help support this mindset.

BEYOND THE BELL WITH GOALS

Goal setting is a research-based strategy commonly used by adults. But too often, it's something people don't learn to do until they become adults. Let's change that by instilling good goal-setting practices in our students at an early age.

Research shows that setting goals is linked to self-confidence, motivation, autonomy, and success. Psychologist Gail Matthews conducted a study in 2015 that showed people who wrote down their goals were 33 percent more successful in achieving them than those who only formulated outcomes in their heads. Students who are goal-oriented learn to become more resourceful by planning and prioritizing goals, and by monitoring their own progress.

You may have set learning goals with your students in the past, and that's a great start. We also need to encourage students to set and work toward achieving their own goals. This is where it gets personal. Goal setting with students gives you the opportunity to get to know them on a deeper level and cultivate relationships.

I like to combine goal-setting activities with get-to-know-you and beginning-of-the-year activities because they go hand-in-hand. When we get to know the learners in our classrooms, we get to know them on a personal level—what they like, what they don't like, where they struggle, and where they excel. This is the perfect time to discuss goals.

But goal setting doesn't have to be complicated or be one more thing to squeeze into the day. It can be as simple as asking a question; for instance, by asking littles, "What's one thing that would make today great?" or "What will make you smile today?" you are encouraging them to set mini-goals. You're also paving the way for success with a positive mindset. The game of school has created a mentality that grades are all that matter, but grades do not always reflect learning. And that's why we need to ensure that goals are connected to learning, not grades.

Our older students will almost automatically associate goal setting with grades. But it's important that they set learning goals that aren't tied to grades. What I mean by that is that we help students clarify how grades reflect a number of habits, practices, and decisions that are within their control, like turning in work on time, remembering to write their name on their paper, and other habits. What is it they will know or be able to do when they reach this goal? If a student wants to make an A, let's talk about what that looks like. We want students to recognize what skills they need to get the grade they desire.

We can use many different Google tools for goal setting, clarifying and documenting goals, reflection, and tracking.

> **Pro Tip:** Use the Google Chrome web browser on all of your devices. Google works best with Google! Even when you are not on a Chromebook, I highly recommend you use the Google Chrome web browser. It is the learning environment for all things Google!

Google Keep for Goal Setting

keep.google.com (A/Z p.23)

Keep is one of my favorite applications, and it's a great tool for teachers and secondary students to use to document and revisit goals on a regular basis. Think of Google Keep like a virtual bulletin board where you can post all your notes and to-do lists. This robust tool syncs with your Google account so you can access it from anywhere, including a handy mobile app. You can share and collaborate on notes or lists, add voice memos and images, and even draw. (Learn more about Google Keep in Episode 41 of *The Shake Up Learning Show* podcast.)

Using Keep to track and review goals is a great strategy for secondary students (and adults). I recommend modeling this for students with examples of your own goals, so they get to know you as well. Add images to make your goals visual!

You could also track goals in Google Docs or Google Sheets, or just about any tool that floats your boat.

Learning Goals

- ☐ Use Google Keep to Track all kinds of goals, including learning...

- ☐ I will be able to define the following terms in my own words and...

- ☐ I will be able to compare and contrast the roles of producers,...

- ☐ I will know what a food web is, what it illustrates, and how to...

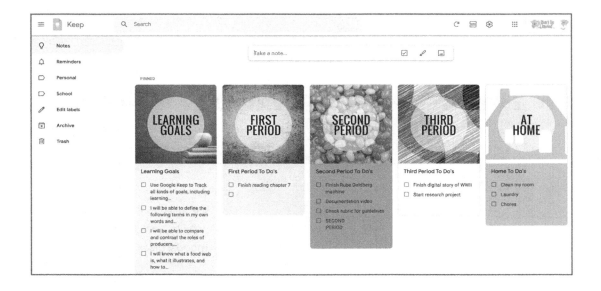

Google Docs and Google Sheets for Goal Setting

docs.google.com (AZ p.27)
docs.google.com/spreadsheets (AZ p.27)

Google Docs is the familiar word processing tool you know and love. You can use bulleted lists and headings for each category of your goals. Make a screen shot of your document, and save it as your desktop image/phone screen so that you can see your goals on a regular basis.

Pro Tip: Try the keyboard shortcut Control+Shift+8 to insert a bullet in Google Docs, (Command+Shift+8 on a Mac).

As adults, we typically associate goal setting with New Year's resolutions. It's true that the most obvious time to start goal setting is at the beginning of the school year, semester, or grading period, but you can jump into goal setting whenever it makes sense for you and your students. The sooner the better!

My Learning Goals

Goals for Ms. Bell's Class

✓ Read three books by December 15, 2020.
❑ I will be able to define the following terms in my own words and give an example of each: food web, producer, consumer, decomposer, ecosystem, population, organism.
❑ I will be able to compare and contrast the roles of producers, consumers, and decomposers.
❑ I will know what a food web is, what it illustrates, and how to create one of my own.
❑ Review and revise my goals each week.

Personal Goals

❑ Create my own YouTube channel.
❑ Read all the Harry Potter books by the end of the school year.
❑ Make the basketball team.

Google Sheets Mood and Gratitude Tracker from Lisa Johnson

	A	B	C	D
1	📅 Day	😊 AM Mood	🌙 PM Mood	💙 Daily Gratitude (a Word, a Moment, a Memory)
2	1	😊 Happy	😴 Tired	My best friend and I had pizza for lunch.
3	2	😊 Happy	😊 Happy	Baseball practice started today! Yay!
4	3	😟 Worried/Anxic	😊 Happy	Made a 95 on my test!
5	4			
6	5			
7	6			
8	7			

Google Sheets is also a great way to track learning goals, moods, gratitude, and more.

I spend hours at the end of every year reflecting on my goals and setting new ones for the upcoming year. (Writing this book was at the top of my list for 2020.) Throughout the year, I revisit my goals at least once a week (and for some goals, daily) to make sure my actions and activities align with my purpose. Which brings us to the next point: To be effective, goals must be revisited at least every few weeks (daily is better), so you don't lose sight of what you and your students want to achieve. It's easy to get distracted and busy with life, only to realize we haven't made time for the things that we really want to accomplish. Revisiting goals needs to become a habit if we want to make attaining those goals a reality.

Goal Setting with Vision Boards

Another great goal-setting activity that makes it easy to keep goals visible is creating vision boards. Vision boards are a visual way to imagine reaching your goals. Traditional vision boards are a collage of images and words designed to help you stay focused on what it will look like when you reach your goals.

Vision boards are not a new idea. You may have even seen them talked about on Oprah, and they were briefly mentioned in my first book. I've been creating them for years. I go old-school and create them with foam board, magazine clippings, markers, washi tape, and everything in my craft arsenal.

One year, as I was creating my board, it occurred to me that if this strategy is great for me, I should be using it with my students. Making this a digital activity made it something students could access and add to throughout the year, and it saved a lot of time on clean up! No glue smears, paper scraps, or marker stains to speak of!

Pro Tip: Bookmark the Classwork page for each of your classes in Google Classroom to save you extra clicks!

Vision Boards with Google Slides or Google Drawings

docs.google.com/presentation (A–Z p.27)
drawings.google.com (A–Z p.18)

Google Slides and Google Drawings are perfect for image-driven creations such as vision boards. These two tools have similar features, but I prefer to think of Google Drawings as a canvas for creation and Slides as a deck of canvases for creation. If your students are creating vision boards, they could easily use either of these tools, but here are a few reasons I especially like Google Slides for vision boards:

- Slides offers the advantage of using add-ons such as Unsplash, where students can find high-resolution photos to add to their projects. Unsplash photos are free to use in any project, and because you can use the add-on to search and insert, students don't have to open a new tab and leave Google Slides—keeping them focused on the task at hand!

- Slides also works well for combining your students' work into one larger class slide deck.

- In Slides, you can assign each student a slide in the deck, and they can work within the deck simultaneously. This will also come in handy for students to later leave comments and feedback for each other.

Vision Board Example from Vicki Heupel

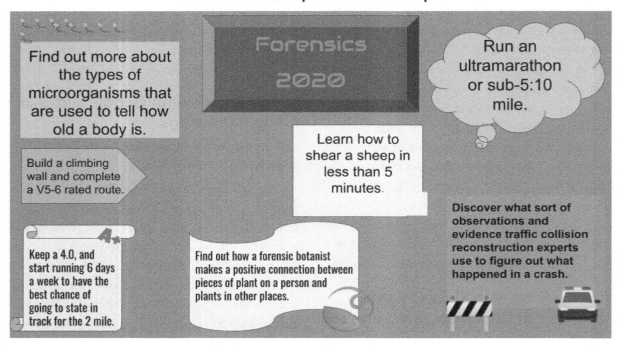

- When assigning a whole class slide deck in Google Classroom, be sure to select *Students can edit file.* (Note: In a collaborative slide deck, students can see and edit any slide. Consider this a teachable moment to talk about digital etiquette and expectations.)

- Or, if you prefer for students to work solo, you can have students create from a blank slide or you can provide a template. When assigning a template in Google Classroom, don't forget to select *Make a copy for each student.*

One great way to organize a class slide deck is to create a Student Table of Contents Slide. To set this up, I create a table on the first slide with each student's name. Then I create a slide for each of my students and include their name in the title of the slide. Next, I return to the table of contents slide to link each name to the appropriate slide. Go to **Insert>Link** (control/command + K), and choose the slide number/name to link each slide appropriately.

Vicki Heupel, a wonderful high school science teacher from Montana, took vision boards with her students to the next level! Don't miss her Dynamic Learning Experience in Chapter 8.

Student Table of Contents				
Jon	Katie	Summer	Jose	Elizabeth
Kurt	Jamal	Kit	Mark	Rhett
Michael	Amit	Christina	Vince	Pete
Laura	Lyla	Wendy	Brian	Peri

Pro Tip: Google Slides has a secret view! Click on the grid icon in the bottom left of your screen to see more slides at once. If you have your entire class working in one slide deck, you can see all your students working on one screen.

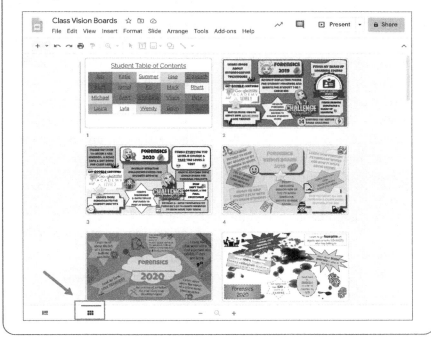

Vision Boards with Jamboard

jamboard.google.com (p.23)

Another fabulous tool for creating vision boards is one of the newer Google kids on the block: Jamboard. Think of Jamboard as a giant digital whiteboard, but better because you can insert webpages, add Google Drive files, collaborate, and well, "jam" with creative thoughts and media!

Make goal setting part of your classroom routines, choosing the approaches and tools that work for you and your students. We want students setting goals for the content we teach as well as goals that go *beyond* the curriculum and the bell. Our goals, as teachers, are to build relationships with students and to instill in them a mindset tuned into learning opportunities wherever they arise.

Vision Board in Jamboard Example

BEYOND THE BELL WITH TRACKERS

Do you use a Fitbit or other smart device to track your habits and accomplishments? If you're like me, you may track your steps or workouts. Trackers can be used to help us develop better habits in any area of life or school and show us progress over time. In my language arts classroom, for example, my students tracked their reading accomplishments, including pages read, books completed, silent sustained reading time, library books they had checked out, etc.

In addition to making incremental progress toward a goal visible, a benefit of tracking accomplishments and behaviors is that the activity helps students establish good habits and emotional control.

Social and emotional learning, or SEL, is an essential component of success for students. Over the last few years, and especially during the COVID-19 emergency school closures, we have seen an increased need to prioritize the social-emotional well-being of our students.

> "Social and emotional learning (SEL) is the process through which children and adults understand and manage emotions, set and achieve positive goals, feel and show empathy for others, establish and maintain positive relationships, and make responsible decisions."
>
> —Collaborative for Academic, Social, and Emotional Learning (CASEL), CASEL.org

Trackers offer students a way to recognize emotions and social cues, develop better social and emotional skills, and show growth over time. By tracking daily or weekly in a Google Sheet, students can see trends in their own behaviors.

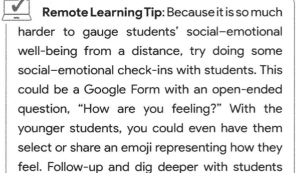

Remote Learning Tip: Because it is so much harder to gauge students' social-emotional well-being from a distance, try doing some social-emotional check-ins with students. This could be a Google Form with an open-ended question, "How are you feeling?" With the younger students, you could even have them select or share an emoji representing how they feel. Follow-up and dig deeper with students who state anything concerning.

Google Sheets for Tracking
docs.google.com/spreadsheets (A̶Z̶ p.20)

"Habit tracking is integral to making goals a success. It is the way that we achieve lofty goals... by breaking those goals down into manageable pieces we can complete daily. Habit trackers are one way to do that. Whether it be studying, reading, learning an instrument, flossing, calligraphy, etc., habit trackers are key."

—Lisa Johnson

In her book *Creatively Productive*, my friend and colleague Lisa Johnson, from TechChef4U.com, provides a number of tracker templates. Most of her templates are available in Google Sheets and Numbers on Mac/iPad. Like Lisa, I love tracking data in a spreadsheet because it makes recording progress fast! Using templates, like those Lisa provides, simplifies the creation process.

Google Sheets Tracker Example from Lisa Johnson

	Leveling Up Life		Goals in Each Category	Do More Of	Do Less Of	Finish	Do Better
2	Family	0					
3	Social Life	0					
4	Sleep	0					
5	Academics	0					
6	Entertainment/Recreation	0					
7	Mental/Emotional Health	0					
8	Physical Health	0					
9	Reading	0					
10	Productivity/Time Management	0					
11	Extracurricular	0					

Google Sheets is a great application for tracking habits, emotions, reading, health, and even moods. Tracking is easy, not too time-consuming, and definitely a big bang for the buck. The templates Lisa created in Google Sheets help us track and document reflection, reading, gratitude and mood, as well as healthy habits. What kind of tracker would be most helpful for your students right now?

Google Forms to Simplify Data Tracking

docs.google.com/forms (A→Z p.23)

Google Forms is another great tool for tracking. It's a simple strategy to create a Google form that prompts students to enter the information for their tracker, and it magically feeds into the Google Sheet. Then we can easily see the data in Google Sheets, analyze the data, and see progress over time. This strategy works for anything you track over time in your classroom. It could be as simple as noting whether they have completed their homework or a milestone for a larger project. The teacher then can see at a glance who has completed a task.

Trackers will also help drive conversations with students and parents. Monitoring the data of your students will give you a window into what's going on in their lives and how it may affect their learning. You also may be able to see where students are struggling and may even uncover limiting beliefs; for instance, many students (and adults) will say things like, "I'm just not good at math," or "I'm just not good with technology." Those limiting beliefs stifle a growth mindset. As teachers, we can work to help students overcome these limiting beliefs by showing progress through tracking.

> **Pro Tip:** Bookmark your frequently used Google Forms for easy access. I prefer to keep this in the bookmarks bar in Google Chrome so it's always one click away. Show this tip to your students, too!

Reading Tracker from Lisa Johnson

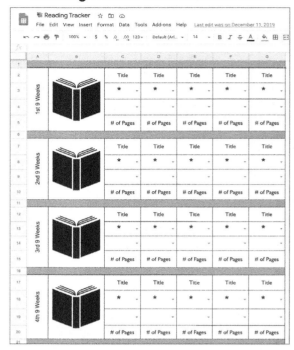

BEYOND THE BELL WITH ONLINE DISCUSSIONS

Start a discussion with students about their learning. What do they like? What do they struggle with? What would they learn if they had complete control over time and place? Remember, going beyond the bell like this is a mindset, not a specific skill, which means it is something you build over time. There are many ways to facilitate this discussion:

- Google Classroom Discussion
- Google Groups Discussion
- Blogger Blog with Comments
- Interactive Google Slide Deck
- Google Forms Survey
- Comment discussions in Docs or Slides
- Google Meet Live Class discussion or 1-on-1 with students

During the COVID-19 school closures of 2020, many teachers and students found themselves replacing a lot of face-to-face interactions with online discussions and meetings. One thing became clear: We need human interactions, *and* we need to be prepared to use digital technology to supplement and support student learning no matter what challenges we face.

Nothing should ever completely replace face-to-face interactions, but even when there isn't a pandemic, online discussions can be beneficial, if for no other reason than to include shy or introverted students in the discussion. That quiet student in the back whom you thought didn't understand the lesson may surprise you when you provide opportunities to speak up in a virtual environment!

Discussion with Google Classroom

classroom.google.com (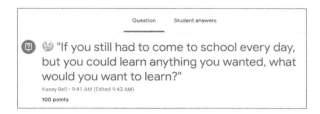 p.17)

Google offers a variety of options for conducting online discussions, including Google Classroom. Using Google Classroom, you can pose questions and allow students to respond and comment. Google Classroom doesn't offer a smooth, threaded, discussion, but if you set it up correctly and set clear expectations for your students, it will work. And it's nice to have the ability to host the discussion in a platform you are already using. To use Google Classroom for discussion, go to the Classwork page and add a new question. Questions can be open for students to see each other's responses, or you can keep it just between the teacher and student for more private topics.

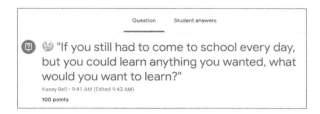

Discussion with Google Groups

groups.google.com (p.21)

The best Google tool for online discussion is Google Groups. It gives you a true, threaded discussion board. Google Groups has been around for years, but it is highly underutilized. As a discussion board or Q&A board, this tool can help streamline conversations and improve communication skills. At a glance, you can see the questions or topics, along with the number of views and comments.

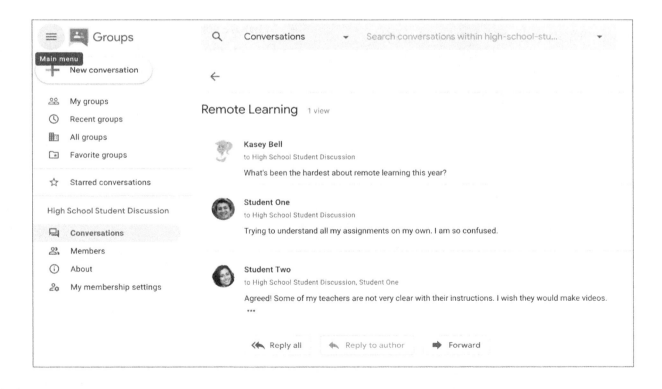

Discussion Starters with Google Forms

docs.google.com/forms (A→Z p.20)

Some discussions may need to stay between a teacher and student. You may not have time to pull each student aside, but you can send out a survey with Google Forms to get to know your students' learning habits and mindsets. Then use these results for quick discussions in class or the hallway, or if appropriate, responses can drive a larger classroom discussion.

Student Interest Survey with Google Forms

docs.google.com/forms (A→Z p.20)

One of the most important things teachers can do during the first few weeks of school is to build relationships with their students. We want to know what they like, what they don't like, where they struggle, and their learning style.

There are lots of ways to get to know your students, but Google Forms is a great way to gather some basic information and keep it organized in a spreadsheet.

The answers to some of these types of questions may not be something students are comfortable sharing with the entire class, so a Google Form is a great way to give students a safe space to share.

Depending on what age you teach, these questions will vary. Below are some ideas to get you started.

- What do you want me to call you in class? (preferred first name)
- What is your favorite color?
- What is your favorite food?
- What are you passionate about?
- If you could learn anything at school, what would you choose to learn?
- Do you like to be recognized for your accomplishments in front of the class?
- What characteristics do you like in a teacher?
- Is there anything that you struggle with in school?
- What do you do if you don't know how to answer a question or problem?
- What do you do if you don't know how to complete your online assignment?
- How do you learn best?
- What do you want me to know or understand about you?
- Do you prefer to work in groups or on your own?
- Do you like to read aloud?
- What are your favorite books?
- Do you enjoy reading?
- Do you like online learning? Why or why not?

Student Interest Survey

* Required

First and Last Name *

Your answer

What do you want to be called in class? (preferred name) *

Your answer

What are you passionate about? *

Your answer

If you could learn anything at school, what would you choose to learn? *

Your answer

What characteristics do you like in a teacher? *

Your answer

BEYOND THE BELL WITH REFLECTION

Reflection is a critical component of the learning process. Often we feel like there isn't enough time to squeeze in time for looking back, but trust me, it's worth the effort. If we don't give students the time to think metacognitively about their learning, we could miss some valuable learning sparks.

Reflection takes many forms—informal, formal, written, or digital—and it may be expressed in a variety of mediums. Several Google tools provide a canvas for reflecting and sharing those reflections when appropriate.

Reflection with Google Docs

docs.google.com (A₂Z p.18)

A simple journal-style entry in Google Docs is an easy starting point. Students can add images, use the webcam to take a selfie, or add links. You also could also use the heading feature with the date if you wanted to treat it like a diary or perhaps organize by subject.

Reflection with Google Slides

docs.google.com/presentation (A₂Z p.27)

Google Slides may not seem as natural a fit for reflection as Docs, but it can be a fun alternative. Let students use slides like a scrapbook to reflect on learning and their own questions and goals. They can layer in images, text, videos, or links, and then easily share their reflections

Reflection with Google Classroom

Google Classroom provides a few different opportunities to support reflection.

- If students are using other apps, such as Docs and Slides, for reflection, they can attach their creations to an assignment.

- You also can use some native features inside Classroom to get quick reflections. If you enable students to post and comment, they can post their reflections on the stream and get feedback from other students.

- Alternatively, you could create a reflection question (open response) and collect answers through Google Classroom.

- One of my favorite strategies for reflections with Google Classroom is to ask students to leave their reflection as a private comment on the assignment.

> **Pro Tip:** Check out Slides Mania, slidesmania.com, for some AH-mazing Google Slides templates. This site has become a fave! You will find an entire section dedicated to education, including templates for lessons, remote learning checklists, choice boards, and more—all for FREE!

Reflections with Flipgrid and Screencastify

Kick things up a notch by adding audio or video to student reflections! Using the recorders built into your smartphone or other digital device, or by tapping into any one of the many Google Chrome extensions, you and your students can easily upload audio notes and videos into Google Drive and insert into Google Slides. Although these are not native Google tools, they do work seamlessly together.

Flipgrid
Flipgrid.com

Flipgrid has quickly become one of my favorite tools, especially for remote learning. With remote learning, we have seen Flipgrid move from that NICE TO HAVE platform to the NEED TO HAVE platform.

What Is Flipgrid?

Flipgrid is a FREE, asynchronous video discussion platform that gives every student a voice. The educator posts a prompt in Flipgrid, and then students respond via video. Then students have the opportunity to watch each other's responses and reply. It adds a layer of fun and collaboration to the classroom experience!

Flipgrid is a great tool for video. Even though it is not a Google tool, it deserves an honorable mention! It's easy to use, and you and your students can log in with your Google accounts.

Screencastify
Screencastify.com

Screencastify is a screen recording tool. Screencastify adds an extra layer of expression. This easy-to-use Google Chrome extension gives students the ability to record their voice along with their screen. This tool allows students to reflect on their learning by showing their work on the screen and describing what they accomplished. Students can record their screen, be that a Google Slides presentation, Google Docs writing assignment, or anything else on their screen, and talk about their learning.

HOW WILL YOU GO BEYOND THE BELL IN YOUR CLASSROOM?

Going Beyond the Bell isn't something simple you can check off of a list. It takes time, but this mindset will affect everything your students do or create.

Before you move on to the next chapter, think about the strategies shared so far. How can you help foster a growth mindset with your students?

Online Resources for Chapter 3

Here you will find resources mentioned in Chapter 3, supplemental resources, videos, as well as new and updated resources.

● ○ **BlendedLearningwithGoogle.com/3**

Online Course: Module 3

Dig deeper and get hands-on tutorials in the online course. This chapter aligns with Module 3 in the course.

● ○ **BlendedLearningwithGoogle.com/course**

Discussion Questions

- As you think about yourself and your classroom, what limiting beliefs are you allowing to limit your progress? In what ways do you need to reset your mindset?
- Looking at the plans you have for your students, how can you make use of some of these strategies to help build that Beyond the Bell mindset with your students and for yourself?
- Which Beyond the Bell strategy will you try with your students?

Notes & Reflection Space

→ (Chapter 4 →→→

Beyond the Grade Level and Subject Area

Dynamic Learning doesn't fit inside a box. Neither do our students. If we're going to eliminate conveyor-belt, one-size-fits-all education, we are going to have to go *beyond* the constraints of traditional subject areas and grade-level expectations. Most essentially, we must give students opportunities to learn about the things that interest them. If we've learned anything during the pandemic, it's that school and learning do not have to fit our traditional models, and they shouldn't.

I know providing broad choice and student-led learning can sound overwhelming, even chaotic, but stay with me here. Students need opportunities to explore their unique ideas and interests. Their wonderings can go far beyond what exists inside the prescribed curricula of our K–12 schools. That doesn't mean you have to teach more concepts, but it does require finding ways to give students opportunities to make decisions and choose topics and projects about which they are curious—even passionate.

Every year, many high school seniors graduate without a clue about what interests them. How sad! How can we expect students to make major decisions, such as what careers to pursue, when they have little to no experience in making smaller choices about their personal education and development? In the game of school, students learn to rely on meeting others' requirements. Over time, their curiosity is squashed; they start to focus on meeting expectations rather than on exploring what excites them.

Case in point: During a professional development summer conference a few year ago, I facilitated a student panel in a school district that was rich in technology. Classes were 1:1 with iPads at the elementary level and 1:1 with MacBook Air laptops in middle school and high school. The panel included students from third grade all the way up to high school seniors.

One of the questions I asked the students during the panel session was, "If you had to come to school every day but you could learn anything you wanted to, what would you choose to learn?"

Immediately, the elementary students started beaming. Each one of the younger students said they loved to draw and would do that every day if they could. By the time I reached the high school kids, there was a distinct shift in the responses. They couldn't articulate an answer about what they wanted to learn without first asking a follow-up question, which usually had to do with Advanced Placement courses, grade point average, or college credit.

That's the result of the "game of school." In this game, grades rarely reflect actual learning; instead, they reveal how adept students are at negotiating with teachers and complying in all the expected ways. This game teaches students that there is one right answer, one right path or formula, and veering from it leads to disaster. Keep in mind, the students who volunteered to be on the student panel that summer were either teachers' kids or high achievers. Some of these students were headed to Ivy League schools in the fall. But they had played the game of school for so long that they had lost their spark for learning. They didn't know how to answer a hypothetical question about their own choice of learning. For more than a decade, those seniors (and countless others like them) had been told what to learn, what to be interested in—and I'd bet what careers to pursue after high school.

We have to find the wiggle room in our days to give students opportunities to explore things beyond our curriculum. I promise this is possible, even with standardized testing and grade-level requirements. Let's explore some strategies to help go beyond the subject area and grade level in the classroom.

Beyond the Grade Level and Subject Area with Student Choice

I'll let you in on a secret: Student choice is the key to unlocking purpose and passion. Student choice is the number one way we can help students find and explore their own interests, whether that means giving them a choice of reading, choice of project, choice of research topic, or a choice in how to demonstrate learning. Every opportunity for choice helps build decision-makers and problem solvers!

To be clear, allowing for choice doesn't mean we are giving students free rein in everything we teach or do in the classroom. And in reality, most students would not be able handle complete control over their learning. But we *can* give them two or three options as a means of strengthening their ability and confidence to make bigger decisions and choices in their learning.

Most students are used to being told what to do: *Fill this out. Read this book. Complete this packet. Turn it in on this date.* In schools around the world, students have been told there is one correct answer. It's in the back of the book, and if you look, that's cheating. But real-world problems don't have one correct answer; in fact, our world needs innovation, new ideas, and creative solutions today more than ever.

As you think about the possibilities of building in student choice into your content area, remember that taking ownership of one's learning requires a big shift in thinking. That is especially true for high-achieving students, who may experience decision paralysis when faced with the idea of flexible learning paths. They'll need your guidance, even as they learn to explore and choose concepts to explore. Ultimately, we want students to be able to find their own way, to become good decision-makers and problem-solvers so that they are well equipped to make choices that serve them well—whether that's in college, in their careers, or in their personal relationships.

Offering students choice and flexible learning paths has helped teachers and students transition to remote and blended learning. Probably one of the best ways to explore this idea is to give students a choice in creating and demonstrating what they know. This will open the door to not only more creative content but also to creative uses of digital tools.

Don't automatically dismiss a tool because you don't think it's perfect for the job. Every time I have done this, a student has blown me away with an innovative idea.

On the flip side, students also need to learn to let go and move forward when a tool isn't working. With our guidance, they can make these decisions while also realizing it's okay to take risks, even if they don't always pan out.

Choice empowers students to demonstrate their learning in more original ways, which, if designed correctly, can also help eliminate issues with copying and plagiarism.

Let's explore some strategies for using student choice to go beyond the grade level. Not all choices go *beyond* the grade level or subject area curriculum, but they have the potential to be dynamic when you give students to new opportunities, ideas, perspectives, and topics, and more ownership of their learning.

Choice of Digital Tool

Have you ever been to the Cheesecake Factory restaurant? The menu there is easily the size of a small book. It's overwhelming! I love all the options, but it takes a long time to choose the perfect appetizer, salad, main dish, and then there's the cheesecake—all thirty-four flavors. It's easy to slip into decision paralysis and ask the server for more time or give up and just order whatever the person next to you orders.

Decision paralysis happens in the classroom too. If you love technology, it's easy to get distracted by the new shiny tools and want to try everything. But hold your horses! Offering too many choices can rob you of valuable instructional time while students deliberate. Avoid overwhelming your learners by limiting their options; for example, allow students to select from two or three different digital tools for their activities and projects. In doing so, you are giving them choice and opening the doors for more creativity. (See how I snuck in another C?) You are moving them toward autonomy and student ownership of learning *and* supporting them along the way.

You can easily embed choice of tools to support the activity; for instance, an assignment in my language arts classroom might look like this:

Using one of the digital tools listed below, retell the *Tell-Tale Heart* by Edgar Allan Poe in your own words.

Be very clear in your directions on how you want students to create and name their files as well as how to attach and turn it in through Google Classroom. Because every student will not be using the same tool, you will not be attaching templates.

 Pro Tip: If students are creating and naming their own files, give students a naming convention for naming their files, such as "The Tell-Tale Heart Digital Story by Student Name." That way, they are easy for students and teachers to identify and locate.

If you have a larger project, you should break-down the assignments in Google Classroom into smaller chunks so students reach each milestone. Or you could use Google Sites or Blogger to organize the assignments and choices in one location for the project.

You may have some ongoing choices throughout the school year, such as choice of reading. You could post a list of approved reading materials on a Google Doc or list them in a Google Classroom assignment. With project choices, consider setting up a Google Slides presentation, with one slide explaining the activity or project, and then linking to the instructions, details, and a rubric (similar to the Google Slides Interactive Choice Board template described later in this chapter). You could also post the choices on your blog, using Blogger or your choice of blogging platform, or in a Google Site. But be consistent with where you host instructions and requirements! Eliminate excuses by creating a one-stop shop so students always know where to find pertinent information.

Remote Learning Tip: When students are learning from a distance, it is even more important to create a one-stop shop for students and parents. Make it easy for everyone to find assignments, announcements, checklists, tutorials, office hours, and more in ONE location. Google Sites is a natural fit if you are using Google tools.

First Steps: Choice of Digital Tool

Don't be tool focused. *Do* take advantage of the suite of Google tools at your disposal, and use them to give your students voice and choice in their learning.

The first time you offer a choice of digital tools, stick to the ones you have already used in your class, the tools with which your students are familiar. Introducing the idea of choice and new tools all at once may sound fun and exciting to you, but it will double the stress and confusion for your students. Let choice be the new idea, and allow students to choose from the tried-and-true tools with which they have experience. Remember: You don't want to lose valuable instructional time as students play and investigate all the new tools while facing decision paralysis.

You may find that students all gravitate toward one tool, and that's okay the first time. Google Slides tends to be a favorite; it's comfortable and familiar. As you mix things up and add new tools to your choice list, eliminate a few of the old favorites from the selections (at least for a few projects or activities). We have to push our students out of that comfort zone so they learn to select the best tool for the job, rather than limiting themselves to the easiest or most familiar ones. Being overly repetitive in the choices you offer limits opportunities for new learning. Find the balance between comfort and challenge that works best for you and your students. Just remember: If you offer the same options in every assignment, you're going to see the same cookie-cutter student work.

Student-Proposed Choice

Allowing students to propose their own choices for tools or devices not only gives them ownership of learning, but it also gives us, as teachers, opportunities to learn about tools we maybe have never used or even seen before. Students have their fingers on the pulse of technology. Being open to learning from your students will help you build stronger relationships with them, so don't be afraid to let your students teach you. I REPEAT, DON'T BE AFRAID TO LET YOUR STUDENTS TEACH YOU!

 Pro Tip: If you offer the option for student-proposed choice, add the stipulation that students must receive teacher approval before proceeding with the assignment.

Open Choice

Each time students choose a new tech tool to support their learning preferences and experiences, they will add to their digital toolboxes. As they become more adept with the tools—understanding their functionalities and limitations—you may want to offer open choice. You might, for instance, include this phrase in your assignment directions: "Using the digital tool of your choice..." Be sure to require teacher approval for open choices to keep students on track.

The Problem with Exemplars

Teachers like to give students examples of the type of work that we want to see. We show work from former students to inspire students, or we may even create a prototype or model of our own. Although providing exemplars is a good idea in theory, the practice often backfires.

Students are so accustomed to following a formula that they'll create one even if you don't require it. I know that in my own class, when I would show an example, students would end up duplicating the example. Adult learners do this too! When I give examples during professional learning workshops, adults often replicate the model.

Let's ditch exemplars! Let your students' minds run wild with imagination, so they can discover for themselves that there are multiple paths to the learning goal.

💡 MISSED OPPORTUNITY

When I walk down the hallways of a school, I see the same Styrofoam solar system everywhere I go—the same project I did many moons ago. Falling back on cookie-cutter assignments is another missed opportunity!

With so many creative tools at our fingertips there is no need for our students to repeat projects from years or even decades past. (I've even heard of students turning in their own older sibling's project as their own!)

Let's avoid cookie-cutter assignments that eliminate creativity and critical thinking! Instead, let's strive to give our students opportunities to be original and tap into those four Cs. As a bonus, when students create something using their own imaginations, we also eliminate copying and plagiarism. Creative assignments are not easily duplicated.

Choice of Reading

When it comes to figuring out ways to embed choice into your classroom, start small, be patient, and figure out what works for you and your students. Reading selection was the first choice I offered in my middle school language arts classroom. Silent sustained reading (SSR), a requirement by my school district, meant students would spend a certain amount of time reading on their own to improve fluency. I allowed my students to choose what to read during their SSR time. They could select a book from my classroom collection, bring one from home, or borrow one from the library.

Some students loved SSR, and others despised the prolonged silence while staring at a page. Some students were excited to select a book of their choice and enjoyed exploring their favorite genres and authors. Others just wanted me to select something for them, and you will find this is true for any type of choice—some students don't want to choose!

Providing choice when it comes to reading is a baby step, but it's still a step in the right direction. Think about that wiggle room I mentioned earlier. Where are there opportunities for choice in your classroom?

Choice of Research or Project

Projects and research are conducive to allowing students to choose their topic. The first time you give students some choice, don't overcomplicate it! I recommend offering two or three teacher-selected choices so that students are not overwhelmed. Break the project down into milestones, and give students manageable deadlines for each step in the project so you can help them stay on track.

Choice of Device

If you have ever been sitting in front of your desktop or laptop and picked up your phone to do a task, you understand this next choice idea. Certain tasks lend themselves to certain devices. Some tasks are easier on a phone, and there are some things for which a desktop computer or Chromebooks are perfect.

In many schools, students are walking around with smartphones in their pockets or lockers. Often we may have access to more than one type of device for our classroom, maybe a desktop or two in the room, carts of Chromebooks, or even tablets. If you have the luxury of having access to multiple devices, make use of it! Help students learn how to select the right device for the task.

> **Remote Learning Tip**: When students are learning virtually from home, there may be more or less choice available. Be sure to survey students and parents so you know what students have available at home.

Beyond the Grade Level and Subject Area with Interactive Choice Boards

I have been a fan of choice boards (aka learning menus) since my first few years of teaching. When I began my career teaching middle school language arts, I taught the way I was taught: every student did the same thing at the same time. But as I improved my craft and implemented things like small group instruction, I learned how to differentiate, offer choice, and provide multiple learning opportunities simultaneously in the classroom. I've since seen how this kind of choice and variety benefits students at every grade level.

Learning menus or *choice boards* (the terms are interchangeable) offer a set of activities from which students can choose. While they are typically more common at younger grade levels, you can use them at any grade level and in any subject area. I have used them with middle school students in the classroom and with adult learners in professional development sessions.

Choice boards can be as simple or complicated as you would like. You can use this tool for a short, twenty-minute activity or a six-week-long project. They can also be used for formative learning or summative projects or a combination of both. They are extremely flexible and easy to create.

A choice board can be a simple list, or it can take on more creative forms, such as a tic-tac-toe board or restaurant menu. My favorite style is the tic-tac-toe board, which is just a table with nine squares. Students only have to complete three activities, and if you follow my instructional design and make the middle square your non-negotiable activity, students really only have to make two choices.

Pam Hubler's All Things Google Choice Board example

Choice boards are not new. They've been around for longer than I've been teaching. Regardless, we can make this effective tool dynamic by going digital and adding interactivity. Including links, resources, videos, images, and more takes choice boards *beyond* paper. Sprinkling in some of the four Cs helps us move further along the dynamic learning continuum to create *new* things!

What Is a Choice Board?

Choice boards are a form of differentiated learning that gives students a menu or choice of learning activities. Learning menus and choice boards can be created in a variety of styles and mediums. They've been around for a long time and originated in a static, paper format. With digital tools, we can bring the menus to life with interactivity and creation.

Why Use Choice Boards?

"...at its core, differentiated instruction means addressing ways in which students vary as learners."

—Carol Ann Tomlinson

Choice boards provide students with flexible learning paths to the learning goal. Every student has different strengths, learning styles, and interests. Choice boards allow us to reach more learners in new and different ways by appealing to those unique learning styles, strengths, and interests. This student-centered tool also allows us to give students a voice in their own learning.

What Do Choice Boards Look Like?

Choice boards can be a simple list, a tic-tac-toe or bingo-style game, or they can get as creative and intricate as you like. Below are some examples

to get you started. You will also find additional examples in my first book, as well as the chapter resource page.

Where and When Should We Use Choice Boards?

- Choice boards are incredibly versatile!
- Choice boards can be used with any age group.
- Choice boards can be used in any subject area.
- Choice boards can be used for short activities or big projects.

Types of Choice Boards

- A List of Activities
- Tic-Tac-Toe
- Bingo Board
- Restaurant-Style Menu
- Learning Style Choice Boards
- Multiple Intelligences Menu
- Four Cs Choice Boards

The only limit is your imagination!

Choice Board Lesson Design

The first thing my eighth graders did when I gave them a choice board was to try to figure out which choices required the least amount of effort. If you design your choice board with some thought and meaning, there will not be an easy way out! Yes, some activities take longer than others, so keep that in mind and try to balance the choices evenly. But most importantly, design each activity to meet the learning goal.

My favorite style to use is the tic-tac-toe choice board. I like it because it is simple to create. Just insert a three-by-three table in Google Docs or Slides. It's great for daily activities as well as long-term projects. And with only three choices for students to make, it's effective without being overwhelming.

When you look at my Tic-Tac-Toe templates, you will notice three things:

1. **I number all the boxes on the board.** Numbering the choices gives you and your students an easy reference.

2. **I use the middle square as my non-negotiable or "must-do" item.** There is usually at least one thing you want every student to do: read an article, watch a video, write a paragraph, etc. This will also control how they make their tic-tac-toe when it contains the middle square. Now, they are only making two choices, which seems less daunting.

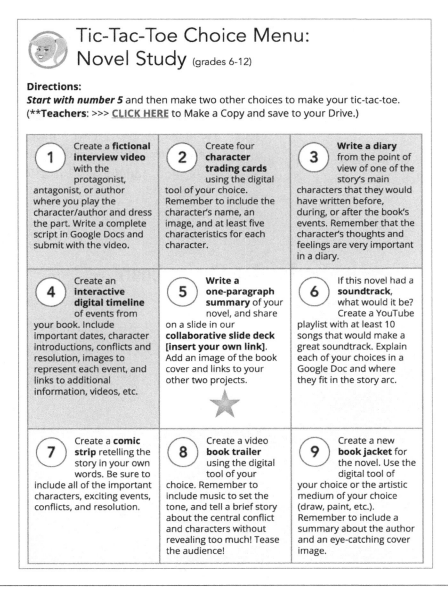

Tic-Tac-Toe Choice Menu: Novel Study (grades 6-12)

Directions:
Start with number 5 and then make two other choices to make your tic-tac-toe.
(**Teachers**: >>> CLICK HERE to Make a Copy and save to your Drive.)

1 Create a **fictional interview video** with the protagonist, antagonist, or author where you play the character/author and dress the part. Write a complete script in Google Docs and submit with the video.	**2** Create four **character trading cards** using the digital tool of your choice. Remember to include the character's name, an image, and at least five characteristics for each character.	**3** **Write a diary** from the point of view of one of the story's main characters that they would have written before, during, or after the book's events. Remember that the character's thoughts and feelings are very important in a diary.
4 Create an **interactive digital timeline** of events from your book. Include important dates, character introductions, conflicts and resolution, images to represent each event, and links to additional information, videos, etc.	**5** **Write a one-paragraph summary** of your novel, and share on a slide in our **collaborative slide deck [insert your own link]**. Add an image of the book cover and links to your other two projects. ⭐	**6** If this novel had a **soundtrack,** what would it be? Create a YouTube playlist with at least 10 songs that would make a great soundtrack. Explain each of your choices in a Google Doc and where they fit in the story arc.
7 Create a **comic strip** retelling the story in your own words. Be sure to include all of the important characters, exciting events, conflicts, and resolution.	**8** Create a video **book trailer** using the digital tool of your choice. Remember to include music to set the tone, and tell a brief story about the central conflict and characters without revealing too much! Tease the audience!	**9** Create a new **book jacket** for the novel. Use the digital tool of your choice or the artistic medium of your choice (draw, paint, etc.). Remember to include a summary about the author and an eye-catching cover image.

3. **I color-code the boxes to align with how they make their choices.** Students choose one option from the blue section and one option from the yellow section. This can also help you with lesson design. Each color can align with a different learning goal. For instance, blue can be research, discovery, and inquiry; then yellow could be creating based on that learning. Or they could all be summative projects.

Another option is to make the middle square a free choice in which students propose their own project, activity, or tool, pending teacher approval. This is not something I would recommend for first-timers, but for students and teachers who are experienced with choice boards, it's a great variation.

Balancing the choices is key and will take time to design. Each choice should take roughly the same amount of time to complete, require equal amounts of rigor and critical thinking, and reach your intended learning targets.

Tic-Tac-Toe Choice Board Templates

Google Docs Tic-Tac-Toe Template

It is super easy to create a table in Google Docs! (If you don't want to create your own, you can use my template, which is available on the chapter resources page.)

Google Slides Interactive Tic-Tac-Toe Template

By now, you know I love Slides! Slides gives you the option to provide even more information about each choice on the choice board. In the template below, I have linked the Tic-Tac-Toe choices to additional slides where you can elaborate, add additional instructions, rubrics, and more.

Tic-Tac-Toe Choice Board

Directions: Start with number 5 and then make two other choices to make your tic-tac-toe.

1. Directions	2. Directions	3. Directions
4. Directions	5. ★ Directions	6. Directions
7. Directions	8. Directions	9. Directions

Assigning in Google Classroom

Typically, students do not need to edit a choice board. Most choice boards are designed to be "read-only." If assigning a read-/view-only choice board in Google Classroom, simply attach from Google Drive and select "students can view the file."

However, many teachers want students to add information or annotate the choice board to indicate their choice, or attach additional work, reflections, and more. Be sure to *make a copy for each student* if you choose this route.

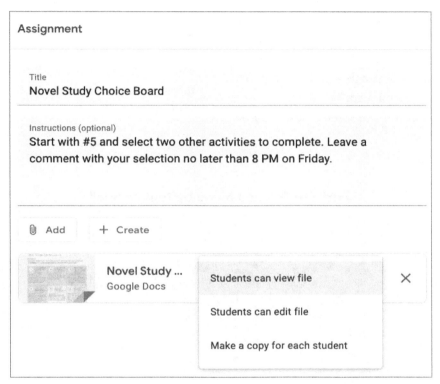

Assignment

Title
Novel Study Choice Board

Instructions (optional)
Start with #5 and select two other activities to complete. Leave a comment with your selection no later than 8 PM on Friday.

📎 Add   + Create

Novel Study ...
Google Docs

Students can view file   ✕

Students can edit file

Make a copy for each student

> **Pro Tip:** Link your Google Classroom assignments in other locations. Did you know that you can get a link directly to an assignment in Google Classroom? Go to the three-dot menu next to the assignment on the Classwork page and select "copy link." Then paste that link in your choice board, lesson, Google Site, email to a student, or anywhere else students may need it.

Themed Choice Board in Slides

My friend, Tommy Spall, from Brenham ISD in Brenham, Texas, has shared many creative choice boards over the years. Below is Tommy's Digital Learning Menu for Student Creation with a Fortnite twist.

In this Google Slides menu, students choose where to drop on the Fortnite map. Each location is color-coded by the type of tool, with the addition of teacher-led options. You can grab a copy of his template and customize this choice board to fit your content and learning goals.

Grab a copy of this awesome template in the chapter resources!

You could choose to engage students with any number of other fun and popular themes or even let students help create the design and theme, while you ensure the lesson design meets the learning objectives. Just think of the possibilities!

> **Pro Tip:** Create a topic in Google Classroom for Resources and Tutorials and keep it near the top of the classroom page. Link to any resources, reference guides, cheat sheets, tutorials, or websites, such as your teacher website, that students may need to access frequently.

Fortnite Themed Menu by Tommy Spall

The Four Cs Choice Board

As we've already seen, the four Cs—communication, collaboration, critical thinking, and creativity—are foundational skills for Dynamic Learning and preparing students to be future-ready. Embedding the four Cs in your learning menus and choice boards is another effective way to build a dynamic learning experience. I created the Four Cs Digital Learning Menu as an example to guide you and inspire you to dig deeper into the four Cs. Take this template and included teacher guide and adapt appropriately for your subject and grade level. (You'll find the template in the chapter resources.)

 MISSED OPPORTUNITY

CAUTION: Don't get distracted by ready-made choice boards and other classroom resources available online, either paid or free. It's easy to get distracted by premade templates filled with student activities and use them without any adaptation, but this is never recommended. Every class is different, and every student is different! Ask yourself these questions before you assign the activity:

- What is the learning goal(s) for this activity?
- Does it align with the learning goals for my classroom?
- What do I need to assess?

4 Cs Digital Learning Menu

Communication	Collaboration	Critical Thinking	Creativity
1. Summarize **your learning** using the digital tool of your choice. Feel free to use multiple types of media. (ex: video, presentation, drawing, Twitter, mindmap)	3. With a partner, discuss the **topic/question**, then together create a digital representation of your thoughts, ideas, questions and reflections. (ex: Slides, Padlet, drawing, video)	5. Using the **image** provided by your teacher, infer what happened in the picture. Retell what you think happened in your own words and expressed with the digital tool of your choice. (ex: timeline, diagram, digital story)	7. List as many uses for a **paperclip** that you can think of in ten minutes. Share with a partner and push your team to think of 20 more!
2. Teach a concept from **this week's learning** to another student using the digital tool of your choice. Feel free to use multiple types of media. (ex: screencast tutorial, YouTube video, diagram, podcast)	4. With your team, discuss possible solutions to the **problem** and develop a solution. Together, create a digital representation of your solution using the tool of your choice. (ex: sketch, diagram, Docs, Slides, Sites)	6. Research a current issue that you are passionate about. Using your research as evidence, craft an argument using the digital tool of your choice to assert your opinion with ideas to solve. (ex: writing, video, podcast)	8. Reinvent **school**! If **school** could be anything you wanted it to, what would it look like? What would you learn? How would you learn it? Create a model of your new school using the digital tool of your choice.

Choice Board Product Ideas

Make sure the activity options on your choice boards support your students and the learning goals. As you craft your learning menu, think about what the activities will help the students learn or create. Also consider how you will assess your students' work in such a way that will tell you whether your students met their learning goals.

Below are some product ideas to get you started:

- Timeline
- Book cover/jacket
- Comic strip
- Newspaper
- Trading cards
- Social media profile
- Venn diagram
- Mind map
- Poem/song
- Soundtrack
- Interview
- Diary/reflection
- Book trailer

- Create or mimic an app
- Retell a story or event
- Public service announcement
- Annotate
- Commercial
- Presentation
- 3–D model
- Drawing/sketch
- Collage/scrapbook
- Interactive poster
- Invent a game
- Instructional video or screencast

- Talk show
- Create a blog/blog entry
- Documentary video
- eBook
- Create a website
- Fake Instagram post/story
- Tell a story with tweets
- Create a TikTok-style dance or song

Rubrics for Choice Boards

Using student-friendly rubrics is really important! The purpose of a rubric is not for teachers to grade, but to communicate expectations. Consider the possibility that you may need multiple rubrics, depending on the goal of the choice board. Rubrics should focus on the content goals, not the technology; for example, the content and learning targets met in a presentation are what should be evaluated, not the number of images and transitions.

Rubrics in Google Classroom

Did you know you can create and attach rubrics right inside Google Classroom? Yes! It's simple to create, reuse, share, view, and grade rubrics for individual assignments. You also can give feedback with scored or unscored rubrics. You can even import your own rubrics from Google Sheets.

Author's purpose (Learning Target Rubric)

Student can identify and explain the author's purpose using evidence in the selected text.

Exceeded Expectations	Met Expectations	Below Expections
Correctly identifies the author's purpose and provides meaningful text evidence.	Identifies the author's purpose with some evidence.	Does not correctly identify and explain the author's purpose.

Choice Board Tips

- Don't allow technology to drive your choice board. Make sure the assignment aligns with your learning goals.

- The purpose of a digital choice board shouldn't be just to integrate technology but to leverage technology to engage learning and help students reach those goals.

- Start small! Students who have never been given a choice will be overwhelmed by too many options.

- And, as much as we like to think that students will love having a choice, many will not. They are used to playing the game of school in which there is one correct answer.

- The high achievers will want you to tell them which choices to pick.

- The students who just want to get their work done will look for an easy way out. Make sure they don't have one!

 Remote Learning Tip: Consider offering offline options for those with limited access or to decrease screen time, especially during remote learning.

Laura Steinbrink, a teacher and tech coach in Missouri, created tic-tac-toe choice boards for her students during the emergency school closures. As Laura described on episode 56 of *The Shake Up Learning Show Podcast,* her students live in rural Missouri, and many did not have an internet connection. To better serve her students, Laura offered both online and offline options. This is a great use of choice boards, even when we are not in the middle of a pandemic. Offline always has its place. We need to remember to give students a break from screen time, create more equitable learning paths, and differentiate with offline options.

If you are not already giving students choice in your classroom, begin to look for those opportunities in your lessons.

Beyond the Grade Level and Subject Area with Project-Based Learning

Project-Based Learning (PBL) opens up a world of possibilities for our students. Whether you are doing true PBL, or jumping into other iterations such as Genius Hour, Google tools can help your students reach their goals.

What Exactly Is PBL?

PBL is more than just doing any old project; it's about learning throughout the entire process.

> "Students work on a project over an extended period of time—from a week up to a semester—that engages them in solving a real-world problem or answering a complex question. They demonstrate their knowledge and skills by creating a public product or presentation for a real audience.
>
> "As a result, students develop deep content knowledge as well as critical thinking, collaboration, creativity, and communication skills. Project Based Learning unleashes a contagious, creative energy among students and teachers."
>
> —PBL Works and the Buck Institute

PBL is all about moving beyond the inauthentic, one-and-done daily lessons and activities that never connect. Now, doesn't that fit perfectly into the Dynamic Learning Framework? Vicki Davis said in episode 15 of *The Shake Up Learning Show* podcast, "PBL is about what you learn while doing the project. It's not about learning a bunch of stuff and then making a poster."

If you are new to PBL, visit PBLworks.org to dig deeper.

Google Tools Can Support PBL from Beginning to End

Using Google Tools throughout Each Phase of PBL

Students can use Google Search for the planning of the project, record and synthesize information in Google Docs, collect and analyze data with Google Forms and Sheets, and manage time and deadlines with Google Keep and Google Calendar. Google Photos can help document experiments and processes. The final product or presentation can be shared through Google Slides or Google Sites, which could serve as a complete portfolio of their entire project.

Genius Hour + Google

Genius Hour is a special form of PBL that is often referred to as a passion project. This idea comes to us from something called 20 Percent Time at Google, in which engineers are given 20 percent of their work time to work on passion projects that will benefit the company in some way. This idea has become very trendy in education and is coined as "Genius Hour." During Genius Hour, students are given a set amount of time during school to explore their passions and interests and learn what they want to learn with a specific purpose. Genius Hour comes in many forms and flavors to fit the needs of a classroom, but it is a great strategy to go beyond the required content for your subject area or grade level. Learn more about Genius Hour in the chapter resources page.

Use Google tools to support each step in the PBL process.

- Use Jamboard to brainstorm ideas.
- Use Google Search to research the topic or problem.
- Use Google Docs to take notes and define the project.
- Use Google Slides to present prototypes and solutions.
- Use Google Keep to manage project tasks.
- Use Google Classroom to assign projects. (I recommend you break this into milestones and create assignments with due dates for each milestone in a long-term project.)

HOW WILL YOU GO BEYOND THE GRADE LEVEL AND SUBJECT AREA WITH YOUR STUDENTS?

Where can you find the wiggle room to give your students more opportunities to learn about things that may fall outside of your prescribed curriculum? No matter what strategies you try, remember the goal is to help students discover new interests and passions.

Online Resources for Chapter 4

Here you will find resources mentioned in Chapter 4, supplemental resources, videos, as well as new and updated resources.

BlendedLearningwithGoogle.com/4

Online Course: Module 4

Dig deeper and get hands-on tutorials in the online course. This chapter aligns with Module 4 in the course.

BlendedLearningwithGoogle.com/course

Discussion Questions

- Where can you offer students more voice and choice in their learning?
- How can you create more project-based learning experiences for your students?
- How can you give your students more opportunities to learn about the things that interest them?

Notes & Reflection Space

Beyond the Walls

When I developed the Dynamic Learning Framework and identified the five characteristics or "Beyonds," going *Beyond the Walls* had two core components: 1) bringing the outside world into the classroom, and 2) empowering students to share their work with a wide (even global) audience. I still believe that every student at every grade should have opportunities to connect with experts and learners globally as well as publish their work for an international audience. But in 2020, going *Beyond the Walls* took on a whole *nother* meaning. (*Nother* is Texan for new, additional, another—all wrapped up in one twangy word.)

The COVID-19 pandemic forced schools worldwide to close their doors. With students, teachers, and parents abruptly mandated to stay home, teaching and learning had to take place remotely. We were not prepared, nor did we receive much training in preparation for school closures. Forced to sink or swim, teachers, administrators, parents, students, and everyone in between clung to Google tools and other digital resources like a life raft.

Amid the chaos and fear, something amazing happened. Teachers accepted the challenge with bravery unlike anything I had seen before. Even teachers who had previously resisted technology got online to make sure that their students stayed afloat and kept learning. There was no alternative; virtual learning and digital communication skills became everyone's priority.

I am in awe of you, my fellow teachers. You were given a brand new job, something no one has done before, and you did everything you could to help your students. The often undervalued depth and heart of those committed this profession is why I love educators!

In the aftermath of the initial pandemic scare, we are all working on creating a sense of normalcy, even though there's a sense that things will never go back to the way we lived pre-COVID-19. Regardless of the challenges we will surely face in the coming months and years, one thing is certain: Going *Beyond the Walls* equips students for learning, connecting, and succeeding in our ever-changing world. Whether you are teaching onsite or online, make sure your students have appropriate access to global learning opportunities. Here are a few ways you can create those opportunities.

BEYOND THE WALLS WITH PUBLISHING STUDENT WORK FOR AN EXPANDED AUDIENCE

Are you the only person who reads or sees your students work? If so, you aren't alone, but as you consider ways to go Beyond the Walls, I encourage you to stop asking students to turn in their work, and instead ask them to "publish it!"

I had an eye-opening experience with my own students many years ago. Something magical happened when I had them publish their writing online where others could read and comment. Suddenly, my students wanted to revise and improve their work. Their words will continue to echo in my head: "Can I revise mine? I didn't know anyone would read it besides you."

What an arrow to my heart! Sure, we would all love to believe that we are our students' favorite audience, but frankly, having an audience of one is about as inauthentic as it gets. Even our teacher-pleasers don't give us their best when they do work simply to satisfy us. But their level of effort and attention increases significantly when we expand their audience. Which is why students should be getting feedback from people outside of their immediate classroom.

Many teachers have yet to try this strategy of sharing student work online for an audience beyond the classroom. After the release of my first book, I received hundreds of questions about this strategy, so let's dive deeper because this does not have to hard or complicated, y'all!

It doesn't have to be a perfect audience to see the impact this will have on the quality of work you receive from your students. An awareness that others will be reading and seeing their work is often enough to make students more focused on what they produce. And when they start getting feedback—the most critical component of this strategy—you can expect to see another uptick in their work.

Before you freak out about privacy and safety, let me say that this strategy can be accomplished without any risks to student privacy or safety. Publishing work online presents an opportunity to teach digital citizenship and safety skills, including the importance of not revealing private information online. We do not need to share student names or faces to give them an audience for their work; in fact, using pen names can be a fun twist, especially for younger students.

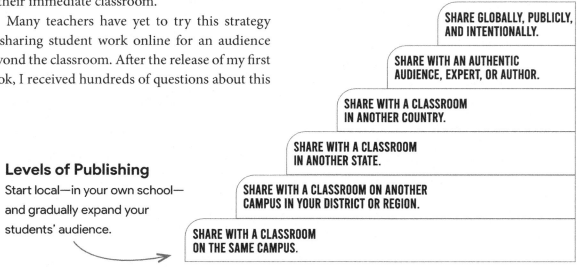

Levels of Publishing

Start local—in your own school—and gradually expand your students' audience.

SHARE WITH A CLASSROOM ON THE SAME CAMPUS.

SHARE WITH A CLASSROOM ON ANOTHER CAMPUS IN YOUR DISTRICT OR REGION.

SHARE WITH A CLASSROOM IN ANOTHER STATE.

SHARE WITH A CLASSROOM IN ANOTHER COUNTRY.

SHARE WITH AN AUTHENTIC AUDIENCE, EXPERT, OR AUTHOR.

SHARE GLOBALLY, PUBLICLY, AND INTENTIONALLY.

Secondary students, especially high school, need to be able to take credit for their accomplishments. Let's face it: Kids at the secondary level are already sharing many things online; it is the way they communicate. Potential employers do background checks, including Google searches, before interviewing candidates. College admissions offices may do the same. What will those searches reveal? My hope is that decision makers will find something valuable about our students that shows what they can do, and what they can learn. I want these searches to reflect what students have learned and created, not their latest social media post.

Tools That Support Online Publishing and Sharing

Most Google applications allow us to share with specific individuals or with a special link. Keep in mind that just because you have made a Google Doc public doesn't mean anyone will find it. To get the attention and feedback necessary to make this strategy effective, you and your students have to be purposeful about how you share work and with whom you share it.

My favorite tools for sharing student work broadly and intentionally are Google Sites, Blogger (and other blogging platforms), and YouTube.

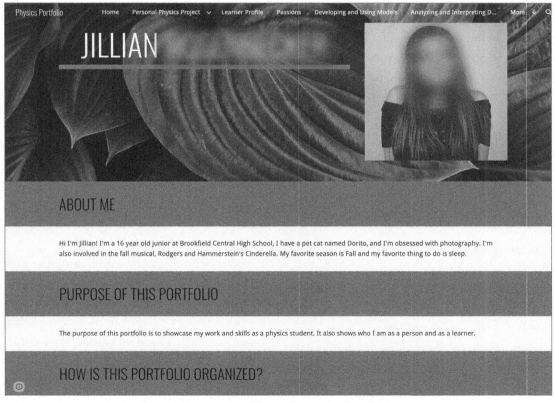

Student Portfolio example from Mike Mohammad

Google Sites for Publishing
sites.google.com (A to Z p.27)

Google Sites is an easy-to-use website creation platform. Sites allows you to easily embed other Google files, such as Docs, Slides, Sheets, etc., which makes it easy for students to embed their class projects on a page. Depending on the age and skill of your students, publishing may look different. With the younger students, K–3, the teacher will most likely be the one posting student work to the site. However, as students' skills improve, the student can take ownership of their own site and publish their own work under teacher supervision.

At the time of publishing this book, Google Sites doesn't have a native commenting feature. Comments are how your students will know that their work is being seen and read. Comments are also how they can receive meaningful feedback, which is what really takes student work to the next level. This is where blogging platforms have the edge.

Workaround: Because there isn't a native commenting feature in Google Sites, one suggestion is to embed a Google Form on the page to collect feedback and comments from site visitors.

Blogger for Publishing
blogger.com (A to Z p.13)

Blogger is a traditional blogging platform. In addition to making it easy to publish content, it allows for comments, aka *feedback.* Using a platform such as Blogger, we can share student work and collect feedback from other students, parents, or experts in the field of study. Comments tap into the superpower of publishing. When students hear from others, not just their teacher but people from elsewhere in the school—or the world—they learn how to write and share their work more effectively and intentionally.

It is worth mentioning that Blogger accounts are restricted to those who are thirteen or older. For students younger than thirteen, Blogger sites must be managed by the teacher on a teacher blog. Students older than thirteen can have their own blog space (monitored and assessed) to share their work and reflections on learning and to respond to feedback.

Although not a Google tool, another platform I really like for educational purposes is Edublogs. I believe students can start blogging as soon as they can start writing, and this platform is friendly for students of all ages. Edublogs is simple for teachers to set up and oversee individual student blogs. It also gives teachers control over who has access to a student's site.

YouTube for Publishing
youtube.com (A to Z p.30)

YouTube, the second-largest search engine in the world, can be a great place to showcase student work and get feedback. Students can create their own video presentations to demonstrate a how-to segment or showcase a science experiment, host an online poetry cafe, or participate in a living museum in which they dress like historical figures and share their research.

Large-group public events are also great for YouTube, and because COVID-19 has forced many gatherings to go virtual, you have probably seen this go-to tool used for streaming and recording events such as graduations, choir concerts, performances, and other ceremonies.

You are probably familiar with some of the drawbacks of using YouTube, including the amount of unfiltered content and the trolls who leave irrelevant comments. Like Blogger, YouTube tries to protect younger users with an age restriction that requires account holders to be thirteen or older. YouTube gives users the option to publish *publicly*, *unlisted* (which means only those with the link will find it), or to keep it *private* so that only the owner has access. You can also disable comments on any video you post.

I have seen many schools create campus or classroom YouTube channels and share student work with great success. You can learn more about YouTube settings and how to set up your channel in Module 5 in the course.

We have so many options for publishing student work to an audience much wider than the classroom. The question to ask when choosing the right medium for sharing is, *What's the ideal or most authentic audience for that particular piece of work?*

If you aren't already doing this, I hope you will try it! In this post-COVID world, sharing is an essential part of learning and staying connected. When you are purposeful and mindful about teaching your students how to share content responsibly, you are also teaching them how to live, work, and succeed in this world. Your learners need to develop these essential digital citizenship skills, so start sharing!

BEYOND THE WALLS WITH GLOBAL CONNECTIONS AND COLLABORATIONS

Let's go to the other side of the wall and let the outside world *into* our classrooms. No matter what you are studying in your classroom, there is probably an outside connection that you can make to enrich this experience. And guess what? The experts and authors you may think are unreachable are actually reachable and happy to talk with your students.

Google Meet

meet.google.com (A_Z p.24)

Google Meet (formerly Google Hangouts and Hangouts Meet) is a web-based video conferencing tool that allows users to video chat, host meetings, create virtual classrooms, and share their screens or presentations.

I've been preaching about the benefits of video conferencing for years, but the age of COVID-19 has broken down walls with a swift and sudden blow. (Hey! You've got to look for those silver linings!) Now, educators and everyone else know how easy it is to connect using video conferencing tools. Google Meet can help expand our learning and connections and break down even more walls!

Let's explore ways to bring the world into our classrooms:

Beyond the Walls with Experts and Authors

In this connected world, most people have an online presence or social account. Those accounts often provide direct access to subject-matter experts, authors, celebrities, sports figures, and political and business leaders. If you are studying a book of a living author, for example, reach out to the author. Many times, all you have to do is ask! Most people and organizations love giving back to education. Be sure to word your invitation in such a way that you are asking that they "volunteer" or "give back."

I've seen teachers' success with this strategy, bringing in exciting experts from around the world—and even from outer space, using video chat tools such as Google Meet, Zoom, or Skype. Did you know it is possible to connect to the Space Station and talk to NASA astronauts from your classroom? During these unique experiences, students get to see the space station and talk with astronauts as they float around, sharing insights about their ongoing research.

Beyond the Walls with Virtual Field Trips

What is your idea of a dream field trip? If you could take your students anywhere, where would you go? Google tools, such as Google Meet, make global, virtual field trips possible and are a natural fit for taking tours or even connecting with other classrooms. Virtual field trips are the next best thing to being there! Students can see and interact with the tour guides, ask questions, and learn about the location—museums, zoos, aquariums, factories, historical sites, and more.

Virtual tours have been around and accessible for many years, and they improve every year. COVID-19 forced many tour-based facilities to close their doors to guests. In response, organizations had to get creative and make online tours more accessible. Looking for virtual field trips for your classrooms? There are new opportunities popping up all the time. Check out the chapter resources to find something amazing for your classroom.

Beyond the Walls with Connected Classrooms

Not only can we bring outside experts into our classrooms through video chat such as Google Meet, but we can also use this tool to connect our classrooms to other classrooms across the state, country, or even the globe!

Mystery video chats are particularly great for elementary grade levels and can be used in higher grades as well. In a mystery video chat, your classroom will video chat with another classroom located in another region, state, or country. Using questioning skills and context clues, students must figure out where the other class is located. Mystery chats are super fun and help students understand the power of connections. What an easy way to get a glimpse at another region, culture, or language, or environment!

Looking for a classroom to connect with? Join the Shake Up Learning community on Facebook and drop a post! There are thousands of classrooms around the world in our group!

 Remote Learning Tip: SEL Video Chats Remote teaching and learning are tough. Think *beyond* using video conferencing tools for learning, lessons, and explaining assignments. Use video conferencing tools to build relationships and focus on social emotional learning as well.

HOW WILL YOU GO BEYOND THE WALLS IN YOUR CLASSROOM?

With so many options at our fingertips, it's easy to get overwhelmed. Stick to what works with your content are and grade level. This doesn't have to be complicated. Start small. Find one new way to break down the walls of your classroom.

Online Resources for Chapter 5

Here you will find resources mentioned in Chapter 5, supplemental resources, videos, as well as new and updated resources.

BlendedLearningwithGoogle.com/5

Online Course: Module 5

Dig deeper and get hands-on tutorials in the online course. This chapter aligns with Module 5 in the course.

BlendedLearningwithGoogle.com/course

Discussion Questions

- How can you give your students a more authentic audience for their work?
- How can you use Google Meet to connect your students with outside authors, experts, or other classrooms?
- Have you explored virtual field trips for your subject area? Check the resource page and jot down three ideas.

Notes & Reflection Space

Beyond the Tool(s)

Next, we are going to dive head-first into going beyond the tool(s). As technology tools have taken the leap from being considered something extra that only the "techy teachers" know how to use to becoming a ubiquitous part of every school in America, using technology—or what I like to call "digital tools"—has forever changed education. Remote learning has forced many teachers to push their knowledge and use of digital tools. We had to find ways to do things that had never been done before. Don't let this opportunity pass you by! It's what we do with these tools that matters. More importantly, it's what students do with these tools that will change learning as we know it. It's our job, as educators, to forge the way.

I like to think of digital learning as a continuum in which we progress from one end to the other. There are many different technology integration models out there, and some are valuable. But I also find that some more complicated models often get watered down for the classroom teacher. Or worse, they are overcomplicated and end up intimidating teachers who don't think they will ever reach that highest level. Let's keep it simple!

We have to think through how an assignment translates into an online or blended learning environment. If there is an opportunity to make the learning more dynamic by trying something new, that's the power of technology. That's the opportunity we have before us!

Think beyond using digital tools to complete only traditional assignments such as papers and reports. Use digital tools to do new things. Just going paperless or digital isn't enough. As my good friend Alice Keeler says, "Paperless is NOT pedagogy."

Use some of these new tools to go further, go deeper, and extend your students' learning. Reach beyond what you think a digital tool can do and should be used for, and challenge your students to demonstrate their knowledge in a new way.

What's most unfortunate is that so many models focus on what the *teacher* is doing with technology. The reality is that what *students* do with technology is what really affects their learning.

I'm not here to intimidate anyone. I want blended learning to seem doable for any teacher at any level, not just those like me who love technology. To avoid confusion or discouragement, let's keep things real and practical. Yes, we want

The Digital Tool Continuum

Using Digital Tools
to Do
OLD Things

Using Digital Tools
to Do
NEW Things

our students to do innovative things in the classroom. But adding one more complication to your plate isn't going to help. So let's just focus on the continuum, understanding that there will be times we are doing old things with new tools (substitution), but trying to push ourselves, and more importantly, our students to do new things with new tools.

Most teachers begin by using technology at the substitution level, and that's okay! There is room for substitution. This book was written in Google Docs, a substitution for paper. The tool supported my work in new ways, too. It allowed me to share the document with my editors, who used comments to communicate and suggest edits. We could even make revisions simultaneously. Best of all, I was able to communicate and collaborate without having to change out of my comfy PJs (I generally do most of my writing before seven a.m.).

As you integrate technology in your classroom, I hope you'll evaluate every lesson through the eyes of opportunity. As you do that, keeping these two questions in mind will help you move toward Dynamic Learning by using Google and other digital tools:

1. How are students consuming information with digital tools?
2. How can students create original products with digital tools?

Look for ways to make the most out of the opportunities that technology provides and be intentional about using digital tools to do *new* things.

Use Digital Tools to GET Information Instead of Disseminating It

We often think of ways to deliver content using digital tools, which is great, but getting students involved and interacting with content is even better.

Instead of thinking how you can deliver a lesson using technology, consider ways to open up your lessons to allow students to give you information, check for understanding, demonstrate their learning, and give and get feedback, comments, ideas, and reflections.

Think of tools such as Google Classroom as more than just an assignment manager. Use your learning management systems to communicate, collaborate, and create feedback loops. (Get the Google Classroom Cheat Sheets for Teachers and Students: shakeup.link/gccheat.)

And as we try to gauge the social and emotional well-being of our students remotely, we can also use digital tools to help students to communicate their emotions. Consider how you can use digital tools for social-emotional check-ins or use private comments to have one-on-one conversations with students.

Use technology that allows students to interact with the information in some way, such as interactive graphic organizers, virtual manipulatives, interactive videos, and multimedia annotation.

> **Pro Tip:** Use consistent naming conventions for your assignments in Google Classroom. Consistency in naming your assignments will help you and your students find what you need. Consider numbering your assignments, and be descriptive, but keep it short and to the point. This will also help you locate associated files in Google Drive. Example: #035 Poe Author Study.

Give Timely Feedback

Instant information at our fingertips means we can assess work and give students more timely feedback through comments, chats, and messaging systems.

Timely feedback is even more important in a fully online or blended learning environment. Google Classroom and other Google applications give us ways to leave comments and feedback for our students.

Consider using the native comments feature in your favorite Google tools, like Docs and Slides, or use the private comments in Google Classroom to give students feedback.

If we only give feedback after the assignment has been completed and "turned in," we are doing students a disservice. Guiding and coaching them toward the learning goal along the way is a research-based strategy that has proved to be much more valuable than just giving students comments when it is too late for them to act on the feedback.

> **Pro Tip:** Use the keyboard shortcut Ctrl + Alt + M (Cmd + Alt + M on a Mac) to insert comments in Docs, Sheets, Slides, or Drawings.

Provide Instant Collaboration

Collaboration between students can happen any time, any place. With hundreds of collaboration tools such as Google for Education, Nearpod (nearpod.com), Pear Deck (peardeck.com), Wakelet (wakelet.com), Book Creator (bookcreator.com), and more, it can be instant and synchronous so that students can work together in real-time no matter the location.

Collaboration is much more difficult in a fully remote situation in which you have no control over the home learning environment. Think very carefully about the purpose of the collaboration and the possible barriers that some students may have, such as limited connectivity, limited or shared devices in the home, etc.

It is sometimes hard to admit that students learn better from each other than just direct instruction from the teacher. Cooperative learning, collaborative learning, and peer learning are research-based strategies that can help students go deeper with their learning and retain it.

> ✓ **Remote Learning Tip:** Try breakout rooms in Google Meet to facilitate collaboration and small groups with your class.

Use Digital Tools for Formative Assessment, Not Just Summative

When technology became more widely available in schools, and a dedicated computer lab was all the rage, most used it as time to type a paper, do research, or create a PowerPoint or brochure.

With so much technology at our disposal today, teachers can maximize digital tools to engage students throughout the learning cycle instead of focusing only on summative products. I see this as a mainstay in many classrooms, even those that are one-to-one.

Even when we consider some of the more tangible products we have created in our classrooms—the tri-fold, the brochure, the diorama—they're still pretty static and finite.

As you are designing your blended learning lessons—maybe completely online, or perhaps you are seeing your students in person—I want you to think about the entire learning process and how technology can help support that learning. Provide additional resources, context, and opportunities to foster communication between you and students, or between students, so that it all becomes part of the learning process.

Use Limitations to Push Creativity

What if we allow students to meet, adjust, and expand their learning goals throughout the school year? For instance, sometimes less is more. Sometimes our limitations will help us see creative solutions that others fail to see. Embrace these limitations, because they just might lead to something new and innovative.

Even when we plan carefully, we can miss the opportunities to be creative in new ways.

Sometimes limitations can force us to get more creative. Students may complain that they can't find EXACTLY what they want for their creations, but when we have limited choices, it can force us to be more creative with what we have.

The idea behind magnetic poetry (shakeuplearning.com/magneticpoetry) is to write something creative and meaningful with a limited word bank. If you get every word in the world, it's no longer challenging.

Maybe you don't have a device for every student. Maybe your school won't purchase the tool you want. Maybe you don't have a lot of time to complete a project. Dig deep for some optimism, and use what you have when you have it. You won't know what you and your students are capable of if you never try.

Sometimes the most creative ideas come out of the least amount of resources.

> ✓ **Remote Learning Tip:** Remember to focus on rigor and let go of the busy work during remote or distance learning. You want to choose the activities that give you and your students the biggest bang for the buck, not simply trying to fill the day with seat time and busy work.

MISSED OPPORTUNITY: WORKSHEETS

There's one substitution and mindset that really chaps my hide—worksheets! What do students think of worksheets? The following image says it all.

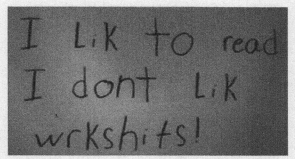

Credit: Jon Corippo on Twitter

Love them or hate them, I hope you'll hang with me here as we take a step back to examine the purpose of assignments, the power of Google tools, and how you can go beyond substitution and static worksheets.

I have been asked so many times how to put a worksheet in Google Classroom that I created a podcast and a blog post titled "Stop Asking How to Put a Worksheet in Google Classroom." Tech integration is not about creating digital versions of analog activities; we have to get beyond substitution!

The term worksheet has become a bad word in a lot of education circles. Worksheets and packets mean different types of work to different types of teachers. As I have confessed many times, packets and worksheets were a mainstay in my classroom during my first few years as a teacher—a truth I regret. I am ashamed that I gave my students busy work so that I could finish grades or other tasks that piled up on my desk. I taught the way I was taught, and in my ignorance I blindly followed the lead of the more seasoned teachers on my campus. What I know now is that none of that busywork engaged my students in new learning, and that was a huge disservice to them. I cringe when I think about the author study worksheet packet I gave my students on Edgar Allan Poe. What a detriment to one of the most interesting authors we ever studied!

What Is a Worksheet?

For the purpose of this discussion, worksheets or packets are activities designed to keep students busy filling in blanks, searching for words, doing crossword puzzles, and other types of work that don't require critical thinking, creativity, or real engagement with the content.

I mentioned earlier that I have been asked countless times how to put a worksheet in Google Classroom. Those requests for help often begin with statements such as these:

- I have a worksheet that I use with my students every year. Now I need to figure out how to make it paperless.

- I got this cute worksheet on Teachers Pay Teachers, and I want to assign it using Google Classroom.

- I have a PDF document that my students need to read and answer questions.

- I teach ELL (English language learner) students who need to practice reading and comprehension on a worksheet.

- I have a PDF article that I want my students to read and annotate.

- I have a graphic organizer I want my students to complete.
- I have a special note-taking device for my students.
- I made one of those HyperDoc worksheets, and I don't know how to share it with my students.

This list can go on and on. Now, let me be clear: Not all "worksheets" are created equal. Some of the activities noted above can be valuable in the right context. Annotating a piece of text or writing, for example, is not a worksheet. Nor are graphic organizers or advanced note-taking devices worksheets.

And if you are lumping HyperDocs into the worksheet category, you missed the boat. You probably fell off the boat.

> "A true HyperDoc is much more than some links on a document. Creators deliberately choose web tools to give students opportunities to engage, explore, explain, apply, share, reflect, and extend the learning."
>
> —Hyperdocs.co

(Side note: Pick up a copy of *The HyperDoc Handbook* by Lisa Highfill, Kelly Hilton, and Sarah Landis. You can thank me later!)

Usually, what teachers want to know when they ask about creating online worksheets is how to put a PDF inside Google Classroom so students can write on top of it. The common, but inaccurate assumption is that a creating a writable PDF is easier than creating something new. Technology presents us with an opportunity to do something different, and sometimes substitution is actually more complicated than embracing a new strategy—like putting lipstick on a pig! I don't care how cute the bitmoji is with your ombre rainbow background. If it doesn't help students engage and learn the content in new ways, it is a waste of time. If you are going through the trouble of shifting an activity from paper to digital, why not use that as an opportunity to make the activity and the learning more dynamic?!

What Is Your Learning Goal?

When I am asked about creating digital worksheets these days, I don't give a quick-fix answer. I ask, "What is your learning goal?" The answer to that question gives me an opportunity to discuss alternative assignments that can make learning more dynamic for students.

If your goal for assigning a worksheet is to teach students how to complete an acrostic, great! But I have yet to see that goal defined in any standard.

If your goal for assigning a worksheet is to teach students how to fill in the blank from a word bank, great! But I haven't seen that goal outlined in any standard either.

But if your goal for assigning a worksheet is to help students learn and understand new vocabulary, I promise you, there are so many more engaging activities to try.

The deciding factor for choosing any tool or activity should always be the learning goal. The learning goal is never the packet, and it's very rarely the technology. If you can't identify how the tech supports the learning, trash it. If you can't explain how the packet supports the learning, trash it! Always choose the tool that will help your students reach the learning goal.

Now, you may be thinking, "But my worksheet helps prepare students for the test."

Maybe. But let's be honest: worksheets and packets are ineffective crutches. Don't believe me? Try this: Before you assign a worksheet or packet (digital or paper), ask yourself:

- Will this worksheet help the learning stick?
- Is this worksheet better than hands-on learning?
- Is this worksheet better than discussion?
- Is this worksheet better than engaging students in new ways?

The goal for using technology isn't to save paper or digitize your old stuff; it's to equip students with the skills to not only pass the test but also to think critically and creatively. Let's use the Dynamic Learning Framework to teach above the test. How can you go beyond the tool of a worksheet (be it paper or digital) and use the five characteristics of Dynamic Learning to create memorable, well-rounded learning experiences for your students?

BEYOND THE TOOL WITH DIGITAL COLLABORATION

Collaboration is one of the four Cs and is a foundational skill for meaningful learning in the twenty-first century. It is also the number one selling point of Google for Education. Even so, I have met hundreds of teachers and students who have been using Google for years that have never clicked on the *Share* button and don't know what it's like to have two or more people typing at the same time in a Google Doc.

If you and your students have never experienced real-time collaboration, make it a priority. This is an experience you need to have. This is an experience your students need to have.

You'll find several ideas and opportunities for collaboration throughout this book, but here's one to get you started:

Collaborative Notes with Google Docs
docs.google.com (A~to~Z p.18)

One of my favorite Dynamic Learning strategies is collaborative note-taking with Google Docs.

Hands down, collaboration is one of the number one reasons to "Go Google!"

The beauty of Google lies in the collaborative features.

When students are able to take notes together, it allows them to learn from each other AND gives the teacher a way to check for understanding.

As a middle school teacher, it was difficult for me to teach note-taking skills, and my students really struggled. They either tried to write down every word, or they got pieces and doodled on the sides. (By the way, doodling is OKAY!)

Honestly, I don't think I really learned how to take notes myself until college. When I was in high school, we weren't allowed to share notes during class. (That was cheating!) If you missed something, you caught up with a friend in the hallway to copy their notes.

Collaborative Note-Taking is a strategy for any age group that is old enough to take notes, usually fifth grade and up. There are many ways to make note-taking collaborative—small groups, partners, whole class, etc.

Four to five students are assigned different categories for the notes, for instance, new vocabulary. Then each student contributes to their assigned category in the notes. The student assigned to take notes on any new vocabulary listens to the lesson or works through the activity and only adds to the collaborative notes when they encounter new vocabulary.

It is less overwhelming when you are responsible for taking notes on only one category or topic. It's also a great way to model note-taking strategies.

Keep in mind, if you choose to do this with the whole class, every student doesn't have to be assigned a category at the same time, but they become accountable.

If the student assigned to add new vocabulary misses something, any student can help them contribute—collaboration.

The beauty of taking notes together is that it allows students to each contribute their own perspective. Something that one student takes away or understands may be different from what the next student finds. But with collaborative notes, we have everyone's thoughts, prior knowledge, and current learning in one place.

This is particularly great for when students get distracted and miss something, because another student will fill in the gap.

We are better together!

This is also a great strategy for professional learning, and I have used this idea in many of my workshops.

> **Pro Tip:** Open a new Google file by using the URL ".new". Simply type docs.new into the address bar to open a new Google doc, or slides. new to open a new Google slide deck, etc.

How to Introduce Collaborative Note-Taking with Google Docs

STEP 1: I create a Google Doc, and build a table inside the document. (See example below.) Tables give it some visual organizations, especially at first. It also keeps students from typing on top of each other. (Tip: If you choose to have more than four categories, change your page orientation to landscape to fit the table better.)

STEP 2: I assign each column a different category. The categories will vary based on what you are teaching. I would break it into four or five categories.

Here are a few category examples to get you going:

- Vocabulary/spelling (all subjects)
- Important dates (social studies, English language arts and reading [ELAR], and other subjects)
- Important people (all subjects)
- Important events (social studies, ELAR, and other subjects)
- Formulas (math, science)
- Resource links (all subjects)

- Steps in a process (all subjects)
- Quotes (reading)
- Anything that you would want students to take notes on

STEP 3: Then I assign one student to each category. I will often pre-populate the table with information I have already covered in my introduction—giving them a starting place and a model.

STEP 4: The rest of the class/group is encouraged to contribute, but those assigned to take notes have the official responsibility. The class will take turns as official note-takers, giving each participant an opportunity to contribute and learn a little more about Google Docs as we go.

Collaborative Notes - Ms. Bell's English Class

Reading: Edgar Allan Poe

Today's notetakers:
- Vocabulary: Jane
- Tone and Mood: Jack
- Word Choice: Jill
- Resources and links: Jared

New Vocabulary	Tone and Mood	Word Choice	Resources and links

If someone sees that another category or idea needs to be added to the notes later, they can use the free space below the table.

Keep in mind, note-taking is not limited to text. Students can insert images, Google Drawings, links, emojis, and more.

Pro Tip: The Google Docs chat feature can also be used as a back channel for the class to discuss their notes.

What Students Learn from Collaborative Notes

DON'T GET FANCY! The beauty of this learning experience is not just the notes and content learning, it's seeing how student collaborate, check for understanding, model note-taking, AND learn how to use Google Docs.

In the image of my notes example above, I did very little formatting. In fact, I only left two empty rows in the table. That's by design.

There is ALWAYS a student (or three) that want to format things and make them look pretty, changing fonts, colors, adding bullets, etc. They, in turn, will show the rest of the class how to format in Google Docs. If this gets out of hand, you can assign one student to format AFTER the notes are complete. Content is always more important than making it pretty!

When students realize they don't have enough space in the table, they will ask how to add another row—or they will just figure it out! Students are learning valuable tech skills as they take notes.

Student Ownership of Learning

Gradually, I give more and more control of the notes over to the students—eventually no longer assigning note-takers. (Yay! Student ownership of learning!)

Eventually, you will not even create and share the guided notes; students will create and share with you!

The notes become what students need them to be, and they are as good as they want them to be.

BLENDED LEARNING with Google

Applying my Dynamic Learning Framework, the collaborative note-taking strategy helps us tap into the four Cs—communication and collaboration. It also helps us go Beyond the Tool by using Google Docs in new, collaborative ways. If you choose, the notes do not have to be limited to one activity; they could live and grow throughout the unit, semester, or school year, which allows us to think beyond one-and-done, hitting another Dynamic Learning characteristic, Beyond the Due Date.

The integration of Google Docs has endless possibilities for students and teachers. Collaboration allows us to be stronger and wiser together.

Of course, many other applications could be used by students to take collaborative notes. I like to start with Google Docs as a steppingstone before getting into other applications within Google or beyond.

The skills students learn, such as formatting, and general style of collaborative note-taking, will carry over into any other applications you want to try.

Google Slides and Jamboard can allow for more abstract organization, and they make it easier to add images and even allow students to embed video.

Give it a try, and let me know what you think!

BEYOND THE TOOL WITH STORYTELLING

EVERYONE has a story to tell, and every subject area gives us an opportunity to tell a story. Sometimes students tell those stories through narrative or expository pieces of writing. Sometimes students share them using images and video. Students can retell events in their own words, students can change perspectives, students can invent and create stories told in brand new ways. Whatever method or tool we use for telling stories, this strategy is sure to create opportunities for powerful, Dynamic Learning—whether you're teaching students virtually or in the classroom.

No matter the grade level or subject area we teach, we need to see our students as storytellers. Kindergartners can create picture books or alphabet books. Physical education students can explain health concepts, exercises, or rules of a sport. History students can retell a historical event. Language arts students can retell a story or novel from a different point of view. Science students can explain the steps in their experiment.

Math students can tell the story of a math problem and how to solve it. Of course, any student can creatively write original stories, narratives, and autobiographical pieces. Seriously, every classroom has the opportunity to tell stories. Here are a few ways Google tools can help you and your students create and share stories.

Writing Stories with Google Docs

There are so many amazing digital tools that teachers can use to support writing in the classroom. As a former writing teacher, I can't help but geek out a little at all the possibilities. But when it comes to Google, and Google Docs, in particular, there are some excellent tools to help teachers and students throughout the writing process.

In addition to the built-in features of Google Docs, we also have access to use third-party add-ons, apps, and extensions to customize the entire Google Docs experience.

72

Writing with technology matters! Students not only need to learn how to write, but they need to learn how to write with technology. Writing with technology will help prepare students for the future as well as allow them to do things that just aren't possible on paper:

- Digital collaboration
- Digital workflow
- See the revision history and process
- Research
- Give them student ownership of learning
- Publish for a global audience
- Increase engagement and motivation

Spelling and Grammar Check

Google Docs has not only a spell-check tool but also a grammar check. Teachers have been asking for a grammar checker for many years, so this is definitely a step in the right direction.

To enable the Spelling and Grammar check in your Google Doc, go to Tools > Spelling and Grammar.

This will allow students to hover over the underlined words and see the suggestions.

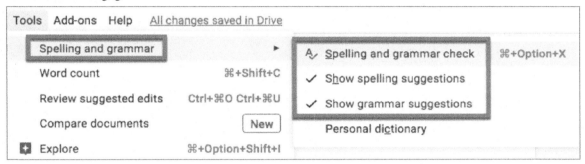

Version History

The version history in Google Docs will show you exactly who did what and at what time! That's account-ability, y'all! Google saves automagically every few seconds, and you can access every change that it records.

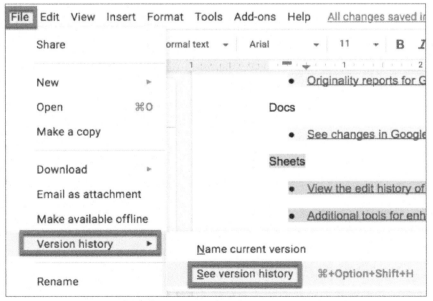

Go to File > Version History > See Version History

73

In the version history, you will be able to see how the document evolved and what each student contributed, color-coded by the user's name and time-stamped! (Be sure you click on the drop-down arrow to see even more detail!)

This allows us to see the writing process in action and see contributions in collaborative work. You can also name versions, for instance: first draft, final draft, etc. Additionally, you can restore older versions if something has been deleted or if a writer wants to go back and see what they changed. Bottom line: version history gives teachers and students the ability to:

- See EXACTLY what each student contributed! = accountability
- Name versions
- Restore versions
- Quickly see new changes

- See whether a student used time wisely
- See whether a student copied and pasted large portions of text!
- See the writing process in action!

Using Comments for Teacher and Peer Feedback

A lot of research supports student collaboration and the power of feedback from peers. Using this strategy in writing can really help students improve, or it can be a big waste of time! For this strategy to work, students need to learn and see good models of constructive and positive feedback.

One easy peer feedback strategy to use and model is the TAG strategy:

- **T**ell the writer something you like.
- **A**sk the writer a question.
- **G**ive the writer a positive suggestion.

When students are writing in Google Docs, make good use of the comments feature.

If you have a collaborative document, be sure to assign tasks and comments by using the "+ or @" followed by their email address to ensure there is no confusion.

You can also check the little box to assign the task, and if students have email they will get a notification!

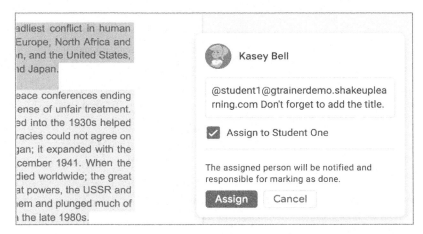

Suggesting Edits in Docs

Google Docs has three modes: (1) editing, (2) suggesting, and (3) viewing. (You will find these in a drop-down menu under the pencil icon.)

Editing is the mode you are most familiar with when you have editing rights, which is the default when you create a new doc.

Suggesting is something special! Suggesting is a way for collaborators to suggest edits and revisions to the document. Any changes are greenlined and appear as a comment out to the right. The owner of the document can choose to accept

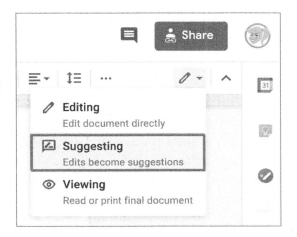

or reject the changes. (Note: You will also see this turned on when you are using the grading tool in Google Classroom.)

Use the Built-in Dictionary

Google Docs is very robust and even includes a built-in dictionary. Students can look up words and find meaning, parts of speech, and even synonyms.

Be sure to visit the chapter resources page for even more great writing tips, ideas, and blog posts.

Storytelling with Google Slides

Slides.google.com (p.27)

Storytelling hits a new level in Google Slides. You can add text, images, video, shapes, and links to create a story that is completely interactive, like a Choose Your Own Adventure story. Students can create individually or collaboratively. Google

Slides gives students a four Cs toolbox, where they can learn to tell stories, gain twenty-first-century skills, and valuable technology skills. There are so many ways that we can tell stories with Slides. Let's take a closer look at some strategies.

Create Interactive eBooks with Google Slides

This is one of my faves, and it was mentioned in the first book. It bears repeating (and expanding), especially as a storytelling strategy for dynamic blended learning! The idea of an ebook is definitely not new, and yes, it's a modified version of old vocabulary, but it can take on more dynamic elements that set it apart from a regular old paper book. I create and share ebooks on ShakeUpLearning.com all the time. It's an easy way to share information. Take student storytelling to a whole new level by having students create ebooks in Google Slides.

What I've learned over the years is that Google Slides is a better choice for ebooks than the more traditional Google Doc.

Slides gives us several advantages over Docs:

- Inserting, editing, and moving images is much easier, so ebooks are more easily illustrated. (If you've ever pulled your hair out trying to move images in Google Docs, try Slides!)
- Add backgrounds, borders, text boxes, graphics, and shapes.
- Design a book cover
- Add links to websites or links to other slides, and make the entire experience interactive! (Now that's a DYNAMIC book!)
- You can make ebooks available in multiple, interactive formats, like a PDF (most universally accepted file format), publish

to the web as a full screen player that anyone can view, or share among students in class so they can leave comments and feedback for each other.

- Kick it up a notch and insert audio—music, sound effects, or even narration!

By the way, Google Slides and PowerPoint are the tools of choice for many of the creations you find (and buy) online. You were just let in on the secret sauce. Just sayin'.

Customize the Size of Your Slides

First, create the customized size for the ebook. **Go to File > Page Setup,** choose **Custom**, and you can create your slides in any size you wish. For an ebook, most likely, you will want 8.5 × 11 inches—the same as a standard sheet of paper. If you do not plan to print, you may consider other sizes.

> **Pro Tip:** Once you realize this little custom size options trick in Slides, a whole world of opportunities opens up! You can create in any size you want! And before you ask, the size you choose applies to every slide in the deck. Sorry, you can't have multiple sizes in one presentation—at least at the time of writing this book.

Add Your Content

Now add the content for your ebook. Create a cover page, header, and a footer with page numbers and title. Make it interactive if you want by adding links to outside resources and websites. You may even wish to add a table of contents, depending on the length of your ebook. Keep in mind there isn't an automatic table of contents generator like there is in Docs, so you will have to create this from scratch. Insert audio, video, and any other content needed to complete your ebook.

You can link your table of contents to the slide/page by going to **Insert > Link** (control/command + K) and choosing the slide number.

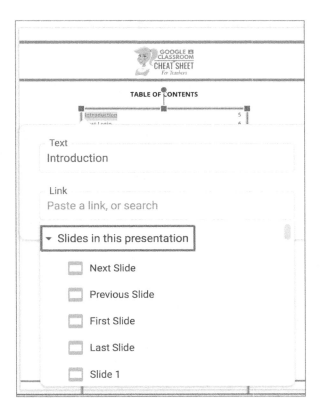

Publish to the web or Download as PDF

Once you have finished the content of your book, you can choose your method of publishing, usually downloading as a PDF, or publishing it to the web to post it online. If your ebook contains audio, video, or animation, you will want to publish to the web If your ebook is text and links, you can choose PDF. (Note: Audio, video, and animations will not work in a PDF.)

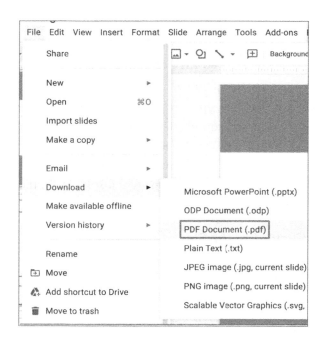

- **To Download as a PDF**, go to **File > Download as > PDF**. Save your PDF in the location of your choice. Now you can share your PDF ebook anywhere you like. You can even upload it to your Google Drive and grab a shareable link to place on your website, blog, or in your lesson.

- **To Publish to the web,** go to **File > Publish to the Web**, and click the **Publish** button. Confirm your choice by clicking **Okay** in the pop-up window. Then grab the unique link or embed code and paste it in the desired location.

Voila! Your ebook is complete and ready to post or share. How fun is that? Think of all the powerful and creative stories that your students can create!

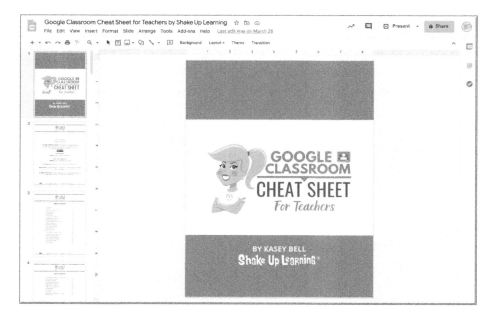

Storytelling with Comic Strips

Comic strips have become one of my favorite activities for storytelling. They are concise. They require students to summarize and effectively communicate information. And they give students an opportunity to be creative with their stories. (See how we worked in those Cs!) .

Keep in mind that when students tell stories in a comic strip, it can completely change the tone and mood. Select your topics wisely so that you don't end up making light of a very serious topic. I learned this lesson in my own classroom, and even shared the story in my first book. Luckily, the topic wasn't sensitive, but it did result in my students learning how to change Edgar Allan Poe from horror to comedy—teachable moment. (Thank goodness that turned out well!)

Tips for Creating Comic Strips with Google Slides or Google Drawings

Google Slides and Google Drawings are very similar tools. Even though these tools are not fancy comic strip generators (going beyond the tool), they give students and teachers the flexibility to create a comic strip with ease.

To create a comic strip template for your students in Google Slides, choose a background color, usually black or a dark color, for the slide and then add white boxes to create the look of the comic strip. You can do this for your students (and probably should if you're working with littles). Upper elementary and secondary students can create their own templates; just remember to plan for the extra time it takes. I find that templates can be a great time-saver for any grade level, you can even use the one provided in the companion course.

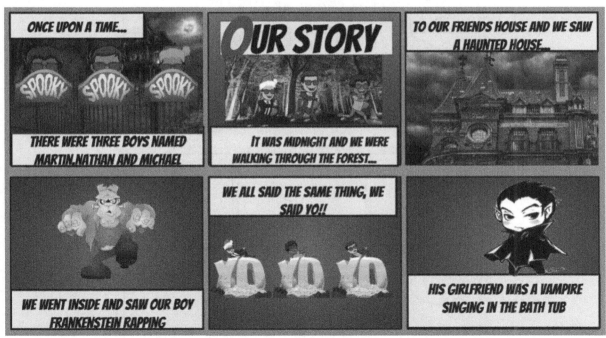

Comic Strip in Google Slides example by Sylvia Duckworth

Keep in mind that the brilliance of a comic strip is that it is a summary with visuals. You don't want the template to be too long, or students will never finish! Limiting the number of slides or boxes they can use will force students to be more creative and will prevent them from spending too much time on the assignment.

Comic strips are one of my favorite storytelling strategies, and these are super easy to create in Google Slides or Drawings. This activity can help students *communicate* original stories, retell stories from their content areas, and solve problems using their *creativity* and *critical thinking* skills. Make this a *collaborative* activity and you could hit all of the four Cs in this one activity!

For more detailed instructions, refer to the companion course lesson or check out Sylvia Duckworth's Dynamic Learning Experience on the chapter resources page.

Once you've shared the template (or students have created their own), students can add characters, settings, and speech bubbles to tell their stories. Before students begin working in Slides or Drawings, have them draft a sketch on paper with the story in speech bubbles and submit it for approval or feedback. The draft step will help keep the lesson focused on the goal (writing, sharing knowledge, making connections, etc.) rather than on using the technology.

(You will find more examples and templates in Module 6 of the companion course.)

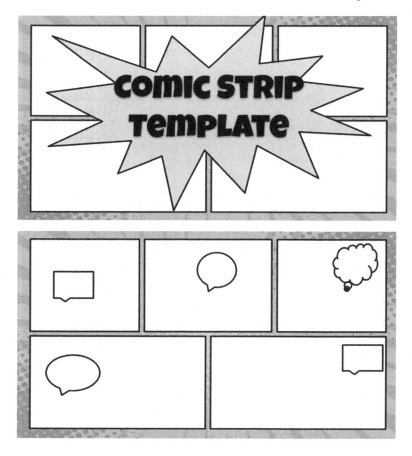

Storytelling with Interactive Timelines in Google Slides

Have you ever considered that a timeline is a form of storytelling? It is a great way to highlight important events in chronological order that tells a story. Educators have been using timelines in the classroom for as long as I can remember. There are many different digital tools for creating time-lines, but Google Slides makes it easy to create a visual timeline, and insert text and information, links, videos, audio, and more—giving students a new way to process information and tell stories.

Yes, you can also create timelines in Google Drawings, or even Jamboard, but I give Slides the advantage here because there are built-in timeline templates. Yep! You heard me—time-line templates. They are a bit hidden if you don't know where to look. Click on **Insert**, then choose **Diagram** to open a sidebar that features several options, one of which is **Timelines**. Select the style you like and start creating your story! With Google Slides, students can add dates, images, videos, and links, taking the timeline to a new dynamic level.

> **Pro Tip:** It's easy to get distracted by the free tech tools that emerge all the time. I call these the shiny objects that distract us from our learning goals. Just because it's new and edgy doesn't mean it's the best tool for the job. Focus on tried and true tools, and sprinkle in the new ones on occasion to spice things up.

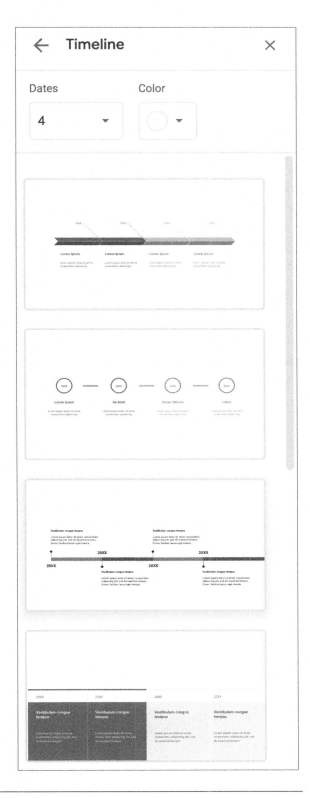

Storytelling with Stop-Motion Animation in Google Slides

Stop-motion animation is a filming technique in which animators bring static objects to life through a series of photographs in which objects are moved in small increments. Google Slides allows us to mimic this approach by using a series of still images. Think of each slide as a photograph (or insert your own photograph). Like pictures that appear to be moving when you fan through a flipbook, the still images in Google Slides are brought to life through stop motion when published to the web and set up for auto-advance.

A really simple way to play with this is to add a single object to the first slide. I usually start at the bottom right corner. Then duplicate the slide, click on the slide in the sorter, and use the keyboard shortcut **control-D** (**command-D** on a Mac). Then on the second slide, move the object a little to the left. Duplicate again, and move the object a little bit more to the left. Repeat this several times. The smaller increments you move the object, the cleaner the final product will animate.

To bring your creation to life, you need to publish your slides to the web This allows you to create a self-playing and looping slideshow that will play your animation over and over.

To publish your slides to the web go to **File**, then select **Publish to the Web**. Click on the **Publish** button, then confirm and click **Okay**. Choose from the drop-down to have the slides advance every second, and select the two checkboxes to have it auto start and restart so that it loops. Google Slides generates a special link with your specifications in the popup. Grab that link and copy it. Then open a new tab or window and paste the link. You should see your animation playing.

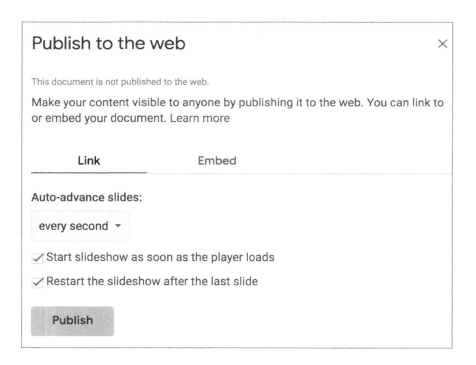

Note: This is a pretty advanced Google Slides technique that may be a bit difficult to learn on the page. Be sure to visit Module 6 in the companion course, and I'll walk you through the process with step-by-step video tutorials.

Let kids be creative with this activity! And remember, they don't have to use clipart. Students could also take their own series of photographs and upload them into Slides. For instance, I've seen students create a story with their LEGOs. Set the scene, take a picture. Move the LEGO characters in very small increments and take a new photo with every tiny movement. Insert each image on a new slide in sequential order. When they publish their Slides presentation to the web, they'll see the story come to life!

Storytelling with Google Photos

photos.google.com (A̲Z p.25)

I love Google Photos and use it to back up all of my photos on my phone to my personal Google account. It's easy to access on any device, and it has some nice features for creating with images and videos, including creating albums, collages, movies, and animations. Students can tell a story using just the application (available on the web or mobile app), or they can import their projects from Google Photos to continue the storytelling in other applications, such as Google Slides, Jamboard, Docs, or even your other favorite, non-Google tools.

Storytelling with Google Earth and Google Earth Studio

google.com/earth (A̲Z p.19)

google.com/earth/studio (A̲Z p.19)

Storytelling with **Google Earth** can be the ultimate trip (pun intended). Google Earth is no longer just for consuming and exploring the globe. If you didn't know it, Google Earth is already full of ready-made stories in the Voyager program. Students and teachers can also create with this magnificent tool to tell stories about our world, using maps and Google Earth.

Go to earth.google.com and launch the app from the web. From the menu, select **Projects,** and begin creating. Perfect for telling stories, like a tour, in the classroom. Use Google Earth to show and tell a historical journey, the hero's journey, explain the setting of an important event or fictional setting, invent your own fictional journey, or tell a personal narrative.

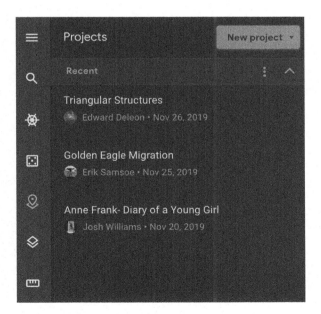

Use **Google Earth Studio** (google.com/earth/studio) to create 3–D animated stories. Google Earth has a massive store of satellite and aerial (3–D) imagery from large-scale geological features to individual city buildings. Earth Studio is the easiest way to leverage this imagery for still and animated content.

BEYOND THE TOOL WITH RESEARCH

When I was in school, we had to do all of our research in the library. We waded through the card catalog, using the good old Dewey Decimal System as our guide. (Some of you may be too young to remember this! Bless your heart!) We jotted our sources and research notes on countless index cards, and just hoped that we had all the right details to create the citations the night before our papers were due.

Research in the twenty-first century looks so much different. Thank goodness! Today we have information at our fingertips ready for instant recall. Yep, researching just about everything is easier these days than it was when I was a kid. That said, the biggest challenge for students in today's world is not navigating the card catalog, it is filtering through the copious amount of information available online.

Citing Sources in Google Docs

Google Docs is an obvious choice for writing a research paper. It is a fantastic tool that supports the writing process with its dynamic advantages, including spelling and grammar tools, the Explore tool, and its collaboration features. But there is another reason to love Google Docs, and it has to do with dreaded citations.

You may remember the tedious practice of counting spaces and memorizing the exact formatting for different types of media. Today's students may never have to do that because they have access to tools that create citations for a variety of style guides. Keep in mind, students will need to know which tools to use and how to verify that their citation is correct. Citation generators are rarely perfect, but as with most technology, they are getting better every day.

Citing sources is a must-have skill for teachers and students, and thankfully, citing sources is easy with Google Docs. I love this feature, and when I demo it at presentations and workshops, it never fails to get some jaw drops followed by *ooooohs* and *aaaaahs*! This is just one of the amazing features of Google Docs that you have to try for yourself.

The Citation Tool in Google Docs

Using the citation tool in Google Docs, students can insert parenthetical citations, save sources, and insert a bibliography.

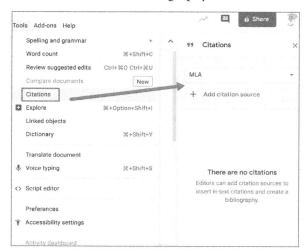

Go to Tools > Citations to open the citation tool, select MLA, APA, or Chicago, and then enter the information to create your citations and bibliography.

Yep! It's that easy! Never again will students have to count spaces, memorize style rules, or suffer through citations.

Researching with Google Search

You probably know that Google Search is the largest search engine in the world, but are you teaching your students how to use it properly? For their searches to be effective, students have to learn how to filter out junk, how to evaluate the credibility of a source, and how to use advanced searches to find the most relevant information. Google Search Education (google.com/insidesearch/searcheducation) will come in handy. This site is a great place to find free resources and to help your students become better searchers, including lesson ideas and best practices.

Research with Google Books
books.google.com (A/Z p.12)

Google Books offers a place to access and read books and magazines, cite sources, translate sources, find similar books, and even set up alerts for specific topics. Depending on a book's publisher permissions, and copyright dates, Google Books allows users to read some or all of the book for free. Google Books is a great companion search tool, especially for secondary student research.

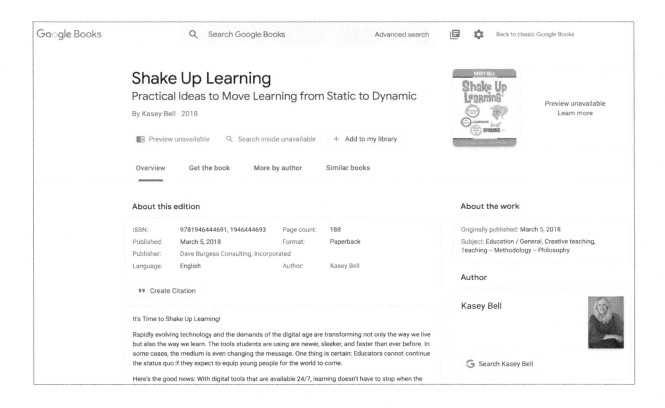

Research with Google Scholar

scholar.google.com (🔤 p.26)

Google may be your go-to search engine, but when you or your students are doing higher-level, academic research, you'll want to visit Google Scholar. Google Scholar is a searchable database of credible literature from a variety of sources, including books, academic research, medical and industry journals, and government sites. Using this site, students can explore related materials, save resources, and generate citations.

Google Forms for Tracking Research

docs.google.com/forms (🔤 p.20)

I'm going to date myself here, but "back in the day," we had to take a stack of index cards to the library to note our research and sources. That seems so antiquated now. As a twenty-first-century twist, and a way to make the experience more dynamic, try using Google Forms surveys in lieu of notecards or just substituting digital paper.

With Google Forms, you can easily create a form with the necessary fields for tracking research, quotes, titles, page numbers, etc., and be sure to add a paragraph entry for actual notes. This form can be created by the teacher, but it will become even more powerful if students create their own, owning the file, and are connecting responses to a Google Sheet. (It's important for students to learn how to create forms, connect to Google Sheets, and analyze data, as we will discuss in more depth later.)

Once that form is created, students can bookmark the live form link in Google Chrome, and then have their notecard form ready to go with just a click.

Research Notes & Sources

Source

Choose ▼

Title

Your answer

Author

Your answer

Notes/Information/Quotes/Paraphrase

Your answer

Page number(s)

Your answer

Additional information

Your answer

Pro Tip: Add the link to the live Google Form to the Chrome bookmarks bar for easy access during research projects.

Using Google Forms and Sheets for tracking research takes the experience to a new level, because instead of trying to organize paper notecards or digital notes, students can now filter and sort their results in a Google Sheet. This strategy collects all of their research, including links to sources and personal notes, in one location and makes it accessible from any device.

Research Notes & Sources (Responses) ☆ 🖿 ☁
File Edit View Insert Format Data Tools Form Add-ons Help   Last edit was seconds ago

Source	Link to Source	Title	Author	Notes/Information/Quotes /Paraphrase	Page number(s)	Additional information
book	https://www.google.com	Shake Up Learning: Practical Ideas to Move Learning from Static to Dynamic	Kasey Bell	"Technology is not a solution, but an opportunity to improve learning."	15	
book	https://www.google.com	Blended Learning in Action	Catlin Tucker	"Blended learning allows a partnership that gives teachers more time and energy to innovate and personalize learning while providing students the opportunity to be active agents driving their own growth."	234	
book	https://www.google.com	Instructional Coaching: A Partnership Approach to Improving Instruction	Jim Knight	"Instructional coaching is a research-based, job-embedded approach to instructional intervention that provides the assistance and encouragement necessary to implement school improvement programs."	4	

BEYOND THE TOOL WITH DATA

We live in a world inundated with data! *Data* is quickly becoming an important component of every job and business.

Did anyone tell you that when you became a teacher, you would also have to become a data analyst? No joke. With the amount of data we now have about our students, assessment results, standardized testing, and other information now available at our fingertips, we should learn how to analyze and take action based on the results of student data.

Not only do we as educators need to learn how to collect and analyze data, but our students need to master this skill as well. Equipping students with the tools and skills to gather and analyze data is a must!

Google Forms and Sheets for Data Collection and Analysis

docs.google.com/forms (𝐴ʑ p.20)

docs.google.com/spreadsheets (𝐴ʑ p.26)

Google Forms and Sheets are two apps that I like to think of as a married couple. They work hand-in-hand: Google Forms collects data, and Google Sheets helps you analyze your results. Google Sheets, in particular, is one of the most feared Google tools, but I promise: It's not scary. Learning how to use its basic spreadsheet features, like sorting, filtering, and using formulas to tally or average your numbers, is a great start to becoming more comfortable and efficient at managing data. Managing data doesn't have to be complicated. You *can* do this!

So can your students.

Here's the deal: Google Sheets and Google Forms aren't only for teachers. Students need to learn how these tools can help them collect and sort through information. If you think these tools are too advanced for students, think again! (And if you happen to be an elementary school teacher, don't think you get a pass on this section; it isn't only secondary students who need to know how to analyze data. So stay with me!) In my first book, *Shake Up Learning: Practical Ideas to Move Learning from Static to Dynamic*, Christine Pinto shared a lesson appropriate for students in grades K–2. It's a lesson she uses with kindergartners in her 1:1 Chromebook classroom. Think about that for a minute: five-year-olds using spreadsheets. I know adults who don't know how to use spreadsheets! Christine has created a self-checking sheet in which students count colored blocks to create

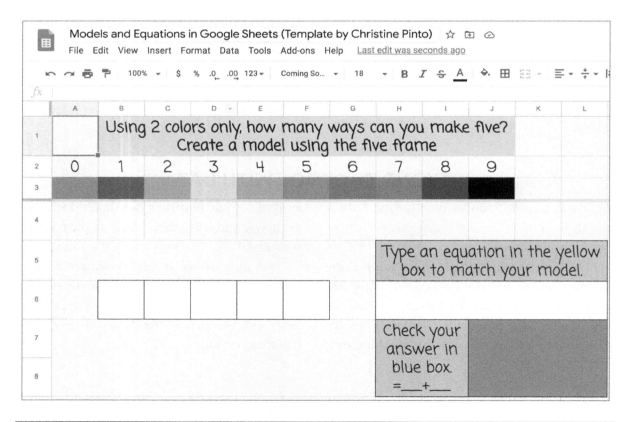

a simple math addition problem—*and* sneaks in a peek at the foundations of algebra. *Ta-da!* They are creating equations! Using formulas and conditional formatting, Christine designed an interactive Google Sheet activity for her kiddos. (For details on the lesson, be sure to visit the chapter resources page.)

> **Pro Tip:** Get free training and tips from the Google Support Center: support.google.com. Learn the basics of Google Sheets, or type in your question in the search bar and find additional support.

Christine is using Google Sheets with *kindergartners*—a feat some teachers assume is impossible. The key takeaway from her story is this: Don't underestimate your students or yourself.

If you work with littles (K–2), try creating a survey in Google Forms. Combine words and images in multiple choice questions so they can select their favorite color, food, or pastime. Then use Google Sheets to create a simple pie chart and talk with students about what the chart means. Simple conversations and examples will set up your learners for success as they continue to learn about data.

At the intermediate and secondary level, teach students to create and share their own forms and then analyze the data. Research projects provide ample opportunities for collecting and analyzing both qualitative and quantitative data:

- Science students can collect and analyze experimental data
- Math students can create and use formulas to calculate data
- Social studies students can collect and analyze survey and polling data

- Language arts students can track comments and responses on the class blog to see what topics generate the most interest

What makes using Google Sheets and Google Forms for data collection dynamic? Remember, dynamic learning is all about going *beyond* what was previously possible. It might have taken a full school year (or longer) to compile survey responses from students in other cities or countries, for example. But technology has made it so much easier to gather information. Today, students can send a link to classrooms worldwide and get feedback almost instantly (allowing for time zone differences, of course!), and use those data in their research and innovation projects. That's *dynamic!*

Voice Typing in Google Docs

As a former Language Arts teacher, I am drawn to the technology that supports reading and writing, so it's no wonder that I love Google Docs. This tool comes fully loaded with features that can save teachers time and save students heartache. One of those features is Voice Typing, and it is a game changer!

This is a speech-to-text feature that is native to Google Docs, and it is available to you and your students as long as your devices have a microphone. When you turn on Voice typing, you can dictate text into Google Docs, complete with formatting and punctuation. Google Voice Typing can also accept dictation in a variety of languages. *Whoa!!*

This tool can be powerful for any student, but especially for struggling students, ELL students, and primary students who haven't learned to write yet, but can speak in full sentences. They all can compose with this tool. This is also a great accommodation for students who struggle with the keyboard, dyslexia, dysgraphia, or the writing and research process in general.

I know, I know, text-to-speech has a bad reputation. But Google's text-to-speech engine, which is built into the Chrome browser and used in the Google Assistant, is fantastic. I can't say the same about other voice assistants. (Let's just say that Siri doesn't speak East Texan. We've had words.)

If you have ever done a voice search, you have seen how well Google understands what you say. Now take this power and apply it to dictation in a Google Doc. This little feature works amazingly well. Think of Voice Typing like your personal stenographer. (Note: Voice Typing also works in the Google Docs mobile app and Google Slides speaker notes.)

To enable voice typing in Google Docs, go to **Tools > Voice Typing**. You will need to give Docs access to your microphone. Then all you have to do is click on the microphone and begin dictating

into the document. (I even used this feature to write parts of this book!)

Reasons to Try Voice Typing in Google Docs

It's a time saver.

Chances are that you talk faster than you type, even if you have pretty good typing skills. Your students are in the same boat, except for the fact that they may *not* have good typing skills. One of the biggest complaints I hear from teachers is the painful amount of time it takes for kids to type a paper.

Voice Typing can save you valuable instructional time. Very few students have efficient typing skills these days. Having students type their essays and research, or anything for that matter, can be one of the most excruciating processes in the classroom. That's where Voice Typing comes in.

I know what you are thinking: *Won't that be noisy?!* Yes, if every student is dictating into Google Docs at the same time it could be a giant mess. But don't immediately dismiss this idea because of the potential chaos. If you work from the position that every student doesn't have to do the exact same thing at the exact same time, you can make it work. To keep the noise level in check, dedicate a time and space for dictating, just as you would if you were recording video or audio projects. Using Voice Typing may not be the way you want students to compose everything, but it's worth a try to see what works.

Tools	Add-ons	Help	Last edit was seconds ago
Spelling and grammar			▶
Word count			⌘+Shift+C
Review suggested edits			Ctrl+⌘O Ctrl+⌘U
Compare documents			New
Citations			
✦ Explore			⌘+Option+Shift+I
Linked objects			
Dictionary			⌘+Shift+Y
Translate document			
🎤 Voice typing			⌘+Shift+S

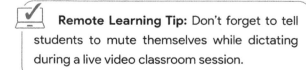

Remote Learning Tip: Don't forget to tell students to mute themselves while dictating during a live video classroom session.

You can dictate and format all types of writing with your voice.

Writing is important across all subjects, not just language arts. So don't limit your use of Voice Typing to text-heavy essays. You can dictate anything into Docs. Here are just a few ideas:

- Class notes
- Meeting notes
- To-do lists
- Starter sentences
- Thesis statements
- Vocabulary words
- Spelling lists
- Word problems for math

You can also dictate formatting and punctuation, and you can correct mistakes with commands! *Yeah!!* Use these phrases to add punctuation to your text:

- Period
- Comma
- Exclamation point
- Question mark
- New line
- New paragraph

After you start voice typing, you can use simple commands like the following to edit and format your document:

- Select paragraph
- Italics
- Delete
- Insert link
- Go to the end of the line

To see a full list of commands, visit the Google Support Center.

Voice Typing supports littles who are learning to spell and write.

Our youngest learners can tell amazing stories. They have the ability to compose, even if they haven't developed their spelling and composition skills yet. With Voice Typing, they can dictate their stories in Google Docs without worrying about spelling or typing. What a great way to support young writers and help them feel successful! Bonus: Dictation can help students learn punctuation skills by learning where to end their sentence and insert punctuation.

Voice Typing supports struggling writers at any age.

Writing can be a struggle for some students, regardless of age. Voice Typing can be particularly useful for those who struggle with dyslexia or dysgraphia, or have difficulties using a mouse or keyboard. Voice Typing is a practical and easy-to-use modification that support students with different abilities and challenges and makes writing accessible to everyone.

Voice Typing can support English language and foreign language learners.

As I mentioned earlier, you can dictate in other languages. At last count, this feature is available in ninety-plus languages!

To change the language, use the drop-down menu above the microphone to choose your language.

This is a fantastic way to support students who are learning new languages, whether that is an ELL student or a student in a Foreign Language class. Students can compose in their language of choice. From there, students or teachers can translate the document into another language by selecting **Tools > Translate Document.**

Yes, I know, translations are not perfect, but like all technology, this feature gets better every day. And for some students, being able to compose in their native language is a game-changer! Even if the translation isn't perfect, it helps to bridge the communication gap as students learn English. It's also an excellent tool for a foreign language learner, who can use Voice Typing and translation to compose in their native language and then read or correct the translated version as a means of studying the new language. Be sure to share this tip with all the language teachers on your campus!

Voice Typing is easy to dictate on the go with the Google Docs mobile app.

Did you know that Voice Typing works on mobile devices? Yep! That means you can dictate on the go. Students can dictate directly into Google Docs, using their smartphones or tablets. This capability expands the use of this feature beyond classroom hours. It also gives you access to the content you or your students have created across multiple devices both in and out of the classroom. Look for the microphone icon on your mobile keyboard to start dictating!

Voice Typing helps us get used to talking to our stuff.

Ready or not, text-to-speech is becoming a part of daily life, which means we have to get used to talking to our stuff: our mobile devices, computers, home assistants, such as Google Home, Alexa, and navigation systems. It may feel awkward at first to talk to a device, but we all need to adapt. And as we all put dictation applications to the test, machine learning will improve in understanding, making voice-to-text features even more precise. Eventually, keyboarding skills will become less essential, because everything will be entered by voice command. The world is changing! Are you ready?

BEYOND THE TOOL WITH IMAGE CREATION IN GOOGLE SLIDES AND DRAWINGS

Google Slides and Drawings are fantastic creation tools. Even though Slides was designed to be used for traditional presentations, we can go *beyond* its original purpose by using it to create products. Honestly, for most creation projects, you can interchangeably use Google Slides or Drawings.

For more details, refer to the Vision Boards section in "Chapter 3: Beyond the Bell."

Think of all of the different images students can create to demonstrate their learning: infographics, memes, captioned photographs or images, original artwork, logos—the list goes on and on. Because both Slides and Drawings give you the ability to layer images, texts, shapes, links, and videos all on the same page, there is no limit to the creativity that can abound.

Beyond the Tool with Graphic Organizers

Did you know you can easily create custom graphic organizers in Google Slides or Google Drawings? Or you can grab a free template from the chapter resources and make it your own.

It's super easy to create a graphic organizer. Depending on what you want to create, you can insert shapes, text boxes, tables, images, or anything else you need. Here are just a few ideas to get you started:

- Venn diagram
- T-chart
- Cause-and-effect chains
- Pre-writing organizers
- Flow charts

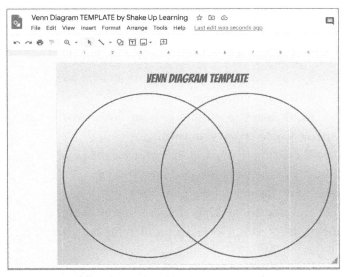

(Check out the chapter resources for some free templates and ideas.)

Beyond the Tool with Google Slides (or Drawings) Drag-and-Drop Activities

Take graphic organizers a step further and make them interactive! Google Slides makes it super easy to create drag-and-drop activities. Students can move objects on the slide to interact with the content. This could be creating something new, like magnetic poetry, the first activity I created.

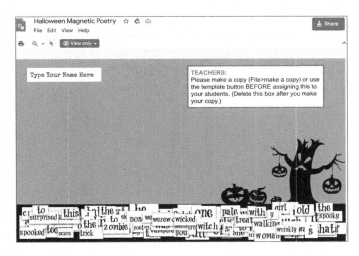

There are many ways for teachers to use this idea to create learning experiences for students.

- The littles can practice counting by moving apples from an apple tree into a basket, as shown in the example tutorial below.
- Label the parts of a frog in science.
- Creative writing with a limited word bank.
- Manipulate shapes and graphs in math.
- Label a number line or timeline with a word bank.
- Use a graphic organizer to analyze and organize information.

Don't spend a bundle buying these online when you can create your own!

These simple tips will help you see the possibilities of Google Slides and how you can create interactive lessons for your students.

The key to making drag-and-drop assignments is creating a background template that cannot be moved. Then add the other elements that students will click and drag around on the canvas. These elements can be images, a word bank for labeling or organizing, or graphic representations of just about anything.

I will show you how to create a very simple example to help you understand the features. You can create activities for any grade level, including more advanced activities than the primary example below.

> **Pro Tip:** Even the most organized Google Classroom Classwork page can become quite long after a few weeks of assignments. Use the keyboard shortcut Control + F (Command + F on a Mac) to search for keywords or assignment numbers on the page. Teach students this trick, too!

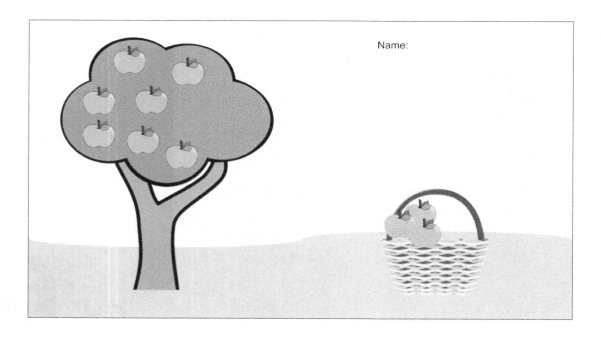

Name:

Steps for Creating Drag-and-Drop Activities with Google Slides

✓ **Note:** Creating drag-and-drop activities with Google Slides can be very simple or very intricate. Depending on what you want to create, these steps could vary.

STEP 1: Plan Your Activity and Align to Your Learning Goals

There are a million ways to use this functionality in your classroom. Before you get too excited and create a super cute background with your favorite bitmoji, take a moment to think about an activity that aligns to your learning goals.

This activity will most likely involve students moving objects, shapes, images, or even images of words into certain areas of a background. That background can be anything you want! My advice is to start simple, so you understand the possibilities, and improve your skills as you go.

Most importantly, choose an activity that is going to help students reach the learning goal(s) for your classroom. Dig deep into your curriculum to make this meaningful and not just using tech for tech's sake!

STEP 2: Create Your Background Image on a New Blank Slide

To keep things simple, we are going to create in Google Slides, but it is worth mentioning that you could also create in Google Drawings. (These tools are very similar!)

Open a new Google Slide deck. (Tip: go to https://slides.new to open a new slide deck.)

The first thing we want to create is the background of the activity. This part will be locked and not moveable for students.

Start with the background color if you want something other than white.

To change the background: right-click (or control-click) on the slide, then click on "Change Background."

Insert the other images and objects that you want in the background of your activity.

🐿 **Pro Tip:** Search for images inside of Slides (**File > Insert > Image > Search the Web**) to find images without leaving the application, which keeps students from getting distracted from opening a new tab to search.

Layer all of the elements you want on your background. Keep in mind the background will remain stationary or "locked" in the activity. We are not adding the moving parts yet.

In the example below, I added a sky blue background, the green grass is a simple shape, a text box for the student's name, and an image of a tree and basket.

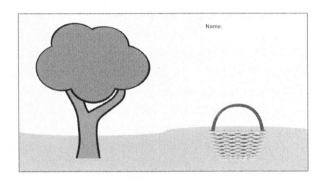

Once you have your background elements in place, go to **File > Download** and download as a .PNG file (recommended for clipart style), or .JPG file (recommended for photography).

STEP 3: Create Your Activity Template

Create a new Google Slide deck.

Add a blank slide and upload the image you created as the background so it is "locked" and students cannot move it around. (Right-click [or control-click] on the slide, then click on "Change Background," and then choose the image you just downloaded.)

Add the elements and objects that you want students to drag and drop, or move around to different areas on your background.

Note: If you want to create a type of word bank or answer choices that students cannot edit, you will need to create these as images in Google Slides or Drawings.

I added the apples and an empty text box over the name box.

STEP 4: Assign to Students in Google Classroom

If you are using Google Classroom, you can use the option to "Make a Copy for Each Student," to create individual files for each student.

You can also use one collaborative slide deck and duplicate the slide template for each student in your classroom. This is a great way to see all of your students' work in one location. And this allows students to comment on each other's work or work collaboratively, depending on the type of assignment.

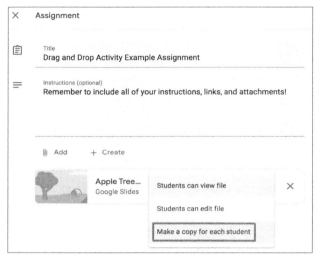

HOW WILL YOU GO BEYOND THE TOOL(S) IN YOUR CLASSROOM?

The possibilities are limitless! You can do so much more with Google tools than most teachers realize. Keep in mind, there's a reason that this chapter is the longest. Going Beyond the Tool is the easiest of the five Bs. Don't get stuck here! These ideas may get you started, but don't forget to go beyond in other ways!

Online Resources for Chapter 6

 Here you will find resources mentioned in Chapter 6, supplemental resources, videos, as well as new and updated resources.

BlendedLearningwithGoogle.com/6

Online Course: Module 6

Dig deeper and get hands-on tutorials in the online course. This chapter aligns with Module 6 in the course.

BlendedLearningwithGoogle.com/course

Discussion Questions

- How can you use digital tools in your classroom to create a new learning experience that goes beyond simple substitution for paper-based activities?
- What stories can be told about the content you teach? How can students tell these stories to demonstrate their learning?
- How can you use presentation software such as Google Slides to create an interactive learning experience for your students?

Notes & Reflection Space

Beyond the Due Date

Remember how we talked about moving past the one-and-done assignments? This is what Beyond the Due Date is all about. You probably read "Beyond the Due Date" and thought, *Um, Kasey, I can't give them extra time! I gotta get that grade in my gradebook."* Stay with me. Going beyond the due date isn't about giving students extra time. Beyond the Due Date is about allowing students to continue the work that interests them beyond the final assessment of the assignment or task, after you've recorded your grade. Thinking, learning, and exploring shouldn't be stifled simply because it was time to turn in a project. Think of this *beyond* more like enrichment and mentorship. You will rarely design a specific lesson to meet this characteristic; instead, with passion projects like Genius Hour, it's easily built into existing learning experiences.

I remember times when my students would get deeply interested in the projects or topics we were learning in my classroom. Now, this was not every student, and it didn't happen all that often. But when these rare and exciting moments happened, it felt magical, and I wasn't about to stifle my students' passion, learning, and creativity simply because my lesson had ended. The curiosity sparked by something they had learned in my classroom was a glimmer that I wanted to fan into an all-out flame!

> **Learning Spark:** A learning spark is when we see a student excited about what they are learning. CAUTION: This may lead to more interest in learning, or even ignite a passion in the student's life.

MISSED OPPORTUNITY

I remember one student in particular. Let's call her Mandy. Mandy didn't get along with many students. She often didn't fit into the status quo. She was seen as different, rough around the edges, and often as the bully. Mandy had a lot of stuff going on at home, and the stories she confided to me broke my heart.

Late in the year, Mandy immersed herself in a novel study we were doing in class. She came in every morning before school, "Miss Bell, Miss Bell, Miss Bell! I did this, this, this, and this last night on my project." She was *totally* into it! She was also going above and beyond anything I had asked of her. I knew she had already met all of the required criteria for the project. But when it came time to turn it in, Mandy asked for more time. She just wanted to do one more thing—something that wasn't even required.

I had to tell Mandy that she still had to turn it in on time so I could get my grade in the gradebook. This was before we had so many devices in our classroom, and it was a physical product that I had to have to assess her work. If this were to happen today, it is much more likely the project would be digital or have digital components that I could assess without having to take ownership of the project. Mandy had to turn it in.

But even though I promised to give it back to her the next day, I had stifled her creativity and that line of thinking. I stifled the passion she had in that project, and that broke my heart. By the time I had returned it to her she had lost interest, and in her mind, she had lost the supportive mentor I had been throughout that project. The physicality of just giving up on something can really be a detriment to our students. Now, every student with passion doesn't have problems at home like Mandy. But for her, this wasn't just learning she enjoyed, this was an escape AND a learning spark!

Think about those sparks in your classroom, ask them about it, encourage them, coach them. When you see a student discover an author or a topic that they are just really into, ask them about it! Encourage them! Give them any extra time you have in your classroom to explore that.

Going beyond the Due Date is also about creating learning experiences for students that live, grow, and evolve over time. With digital learning tools at our fingertips, we can let go of the one-and-done mindset and build project-based learning opportunities for students. Think about more long-term projects in which students can continue to build on their skills and contribute to ongoing projects throughout the year.

Consider a project on inspiring historical figures, both past and present, in which students create a collaborative website to share their research and learning. This project can continue to grow throughout the school year as students discover new and inspiring historical figures in and out of class. A student may learn about someone on the news, Netflix, or the internet, like Steve Jobs. Then propose that Steve Jobs be added to their inspiring historical figures website. That brings about an ongoing conversation about what defines an inspiring historical figure and, if Jobs fits the project, allowing students to connect the past and present.

Think carefully about the power of Google tools that are available 24/7. Consider a Google Doc as a living document that students can add to throughout the year. The learning can live and grow, not only beyond the bell, but beyond the due date.

Let me be clear. Beyond the Due Date is not about giving students extra time to finish assignments. That's a discussion for another day. This is about seizing opportunities! Don't you wish all your students were so excited to learn? I wish I had seized this opportunity with Mandy!

The other thing to know about this Dynamic Learning characteristic is that it is rarely something that is the complete focus of your lesson, but it can easily be embedded in PBL or student choice, and especially in Genius Hour. It is more about capitalizing on the learning sparks we find in our students.

BEYOND THE DUE DATE WITH STUDENT PORTFOLIOS

As discussed in Chapter 6, we can go Beyond the Tools with student portfolios. We can also use portfolios to go Beyond the Due Date as a project that lives and grows throughout the year. Student Portfolios are the epitome of Dynamic Learning and Going beyond the Due Date because they are never "done." As students learn and grow throughout the year, new work is added to their portfolio to showcase their best work or to show growth over time.

For details on tools and ideas, refer back to Chapter 6.

I love student portfolios because they allow us to celebrate student achievement, see progress and growth, and if you choose, share it with the world for feedback—taking this Beyond the Walls as well.

Reflection

Reflection is one of the most beneficial aspects of student portfolios. Not only are they collecting artifacts that demonstrate learning, but students are also reflecting on each artifact along the way. Sharing their reflections adds to the learning of every student who reads and views another student's portfolio.

Types of Student Portfolios

There are many different types of portfolios and many different ways to use this strategy in the K–12 classroom and beyond. Portfolios have been around for decades and harken back to paper files and notebooks, but today's digital versions are much easier to manage and share.

Student Showcase Portfolio

Showcase portfolios are a great starting place! A showcase portfolio is a place for students to present artifacts that show mastery of standards or skills. Showcase portfolios work especially well as summative assessments at the end of a grading cycle or semester. Because these are cumulative, they don't require as much updating throughout the year like some of the other types.

Just like everything, plan portfolios with purpose! Begin by selecting which standards, learning goals, or skills these portfolios will represent. In Mike Mohammad's first iteration of the student portfolio, his students presented artifacts that demonstrated the 4 Cs, future-ready technical skills, and met content-area standards.

The process of creating a portfolio is not merely putting in a title on a page and inserting an artifact. The goal is for students to be able to explain the standard they are addressing. Then students present their evidence with context and explain how it meets the standard.

For any skill or standard students are being asked to address, teachers should ensure that learners have a variety of potential artifacts from which to choose. This forces students to think about what work they did that best demonstrates that skill or standard.

Student Learning Portfolio (Growth over Time)

Another type of a portfolio is a learning portfolio in which students track and reflect on the learning process. This type of portfolio requires maintenance and regular updates by the student or teacher. Be sure you plan time each week for students to add new artifacts and reflection.

Mike suggests designing the learning portfolio into pages for each unit of study. Students place work from the unit and introduce the piece.

This can also be a place for students to reflect on formative assessments such as quizzes. By scrolling down the page, you can track student progress through the unit assessment, including final reflections on the unit.

One of the aspects of this type of portfolio that challenges students most is the deep reflection required. Over time, however, they will see the benefits of reflecting on their performance. Part of a powerful reflection is not just reviewing past performance but using that insight as a platform to plan future action.

Learner Profile Portfolio

If a portfolio is going to be more than a file cabinet for student work, it must not only reflect the work students do but also encompass aspects of them as individuals. As outlined by the Institute for Personalized Learning, a learner profile contains demographic and academic information. It also houses information on a student's skill sets and drivers for learning. In their learner profile

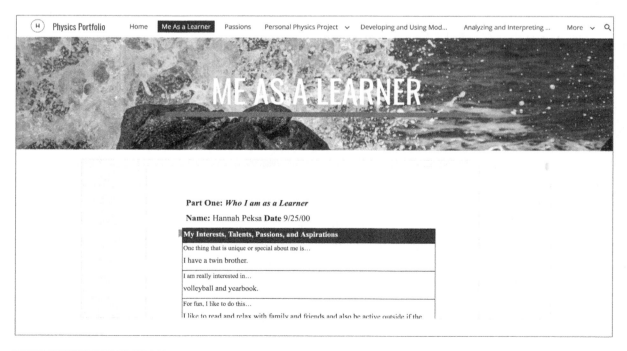

portfolios, Mike has students include a "Me as a Learner" page to communicate their learning strengths and provide evidential artifacts of those strengths. I also suggest you have students include information about their interests and aspirations on a "Passion Page" where they can incorporate photos and videos.

Mike encourages his students to continue sharing their work and passions even after they leave his classroom.

When students are ready to share their portfolio, they have several options. They can share the site much like they would a Google file, giving view rights to specific individuals. If students want to publish their work, they can publish to a specific domain or to the world.

Google Tools for Student Portfolios

Google Sites is the perfect tool for student portfolios. As I mentioned earlier, Google Sites makes it easy to embed work created in other Google applications, such as Docs, Slides, and Sheets. The easy-to-use platform gives a professional look and consistency for students to follow a given format or template. An added benefit of using Google Sites for portfolios is that as students are learning the skills of creating a portfolio, they are also learning web design skills.

Blogger is another a great choice for teachers to manage portfolios or for students age thirteen or older to manage their own portfolios and publishing. What I like about Blogger is that it allows for comments so students can get feedback very easily.

For a more simplistic version, you could consider using **Google Slides**. It doesn't allow embedding files like Sites and Blogger does, but you can add links, images, and video. Think of a Slides portfolio like a container or flip folder, rather than a presentation tool for the end product.

A student portfolio should definitely go beyond one-and-done. These are long-term projects; Mike encourages his students to maintain and add to their portfolios even after they leave his class. It is the perfect project for students who finish assignments early, have extra time, or need enrichment. But it's even better for students who need time and encouragement to find what they love. That was Mandy. Mandy needed encouragement, and she needed to find something she loved.

BEYOND THE DUE DATE WITH MENTORSHIP AND COACHING

Not every student has free time or gets to do enrichment activities. Every student doesn't finish their work on time. But this doesn't mean we can't find sparks of interest. Once we have identified those sparks in our students, we can take on the role of a coach or mentor. This is an opportunity we don't want to miss!

One of the best ways to cultivate passions within our students is through coaching and mentoring. When we find out what interests our students, we can talk about it with them in informal and natural settings. A simple conversation, even if it is only a few seconds in the hallway, shows that you care enough to check in, which helps build relationships and fan the flame of your student's learning spark; for instance, I may ask a student whether they read the book I recommended, visited a website I shared, or connected with a student with the same interest. We can continue to share resources to help the student take their learning further.

- Did you read that other book by Gary Paulsen?
- Did you watch that YouTube tutorial on stop-motion animation?
- Did you check out the coding projects online?

Just encouraging students and helping them find their passions can be a game-changer for many kiddos. Connecting students with others who share common interests can not only spark learning, but potentially, friendships. You may have one student in first period who is interested in coding, and another student in sixth period who is skilled at coding. Do they know each other? Could they be friends?

Starting in elementary school, it's important to encourage students to explore and discuss their interests, even their favorite color. Set up the conversation so students understand that everyone is different and it's okay to like different things—animals, food, etc. This encouragement helps learners discover and articulate what interests them. Once they've found an interest, fan that flame!

How will you take your lessons *beyond* what was previously possible? Don't worry about always being at the highest level. Stay focused on your learning goals and start where you are. Remember: Your classroom doesn't have to look like anyone else's. What's important is that you tap into your strengths and your students' interests to provide ample opportunities for Dynamic Learning. How will you take learning to the next level in your classroom? How will you use these opportunities to build a growth mindset with your students? (See what I did there? It circles back to our first Beyond—Beyond the Bell—and building a lifelong learning mindset in students.)

BLENDED LEARNING WITH GOOGLE TOOLKIT©

I have a special toolkit of ideas that I have put together just for the readers of this book! I call it the Blended Learning with Google Toolkit. This toolkit will bring together the Dynamic Learning Characteristics with classroom tasks and a suggested list of Google tools for each task. Think of this as your cheat sheet for the book!

Get the Blended Learning with Google Toolkit:

BlendedLearningwithGoogle.com/toolkit

Online Resources for Chapter 7

 Here you will find resources mentioned in Chapter 7, supplemental resources, videos, as well as new and updated resources.

○ **BlendedLearningwithGoogle.com/7**

Online Course: Module 7

Dig deeper and get hands-on tutorials in the online course. This chapter aligns with Module 7 in the course.

○ **BlendedLearningwithGoogle.com/course**

Discussion Questions

- How can you use Beyond the Due Date strategies such as portfolios to engage your students and allow them to demonstrate learning and growth?
- How can you capitalize on learning sparks to encourage and mentor students?
- How often do your students reflect on their learning? How can you improve this process and use this strategy more consistently?

Notes & Reflection Space

Planning and Implementation

've given you the tools and the ideas. Now it's time to plan! Don't dismiss the power of purposeful planning, and remember it is part of the Dynamic Learning Model.

> "Give me six hours to chop down a tree and I will spend the first four sharpening the axe."
>
> —Abraham Lincoln

Don't skip this step! You can save yourself from frustration and losing valuable instructional time by taking the time to carefully plan your lessons.

It's easy to get excited and distracted by new ideas, and shiny digital tools, but we must keep our eyes on the prize—the learning targets. In this last section of the book, we will look at example lesson plans, planning questions, and templates to help you take the next steps to plan and implement your very own Dynamic Blended Learning Experience.

Dynamic Blended Learning in Action

If you've made it this far, I beg of you to keep going. This is quite possibly the most important chapter. One of my pet peeves is a book that is all about lofty ideas and perfect classroom scenarios with zero focus on how to implement. None of the other chapters mean anything if you don't take time to plan for your classroom. That's why I've called in reinforcements—my best teacher friends. In this chapter, you will find REAL lesson plans, or what I call Dynamic Learning Experiences. These are lesson plans that have been implemented successfully by some of the best teachers I know.

I hope these lessons inspire you! Explore these with an open mind, no matter what grade level or subject area you teach. We can all learn from one another!

Please note, the summaries for each lesson are available below. Please use the shortened link or QR code to access the entire plan, including assessment strategies, rubrics, templates, and more.

DYNAMIC LEARNING EXPERIENCE EXAMPLES (LESSON PLANS)

Goal Setting with Vision Boards by Vicki Heupel

Shakeup.link/vision
Grade Levels: 6–12
Subjects: Applicable in any content area
Google Tools: Google Slides, Google Classroom, and Google Sites

Dynamic Learning Characteristics

☑ Beyond the Bell   ☑ Beyond the Walls
☑ Beyond the Subject or Grade Level   ☑ Beyond the Due Date
☑ Beyond the Tools

Summary: In this learning experience, high school teacher Vicki Heupel shows us how to take vision boards (discussed in Chapter 3) to a whole new level. Students get an overview of the class or course, a list of skills that will be taught, as well as a list of associated topics. After a KWL (what I know, want to know, learned) brainstorming session, students choose three to five skills or topics that interest them. Students then create digital vision boards to visually represent their personal and class goals. Vicki suggests they include two to four of each type of goal. Although this learning experience was implemented at the high school level, it can definitely be revised for students in younger grades.

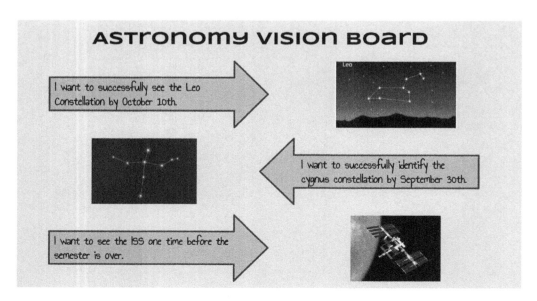

ISTE Standards

- Students articulate and set personal learning goals, develop strategies leveraging technology to achieve them, and reflect on the learning process itself to improve learning outcomes.
- Students create original works or responsibly repurpose or remix digital resources into new creations.
- Students communicate complex ideas clearly and effectively by creating or using a variety of digital objects, such as visualizations, models, or simulations.
- Students publish or present content that customizes the message and medium for their intended audiences.

4 Cs

- **Creativity:** Slides is normally a presentation tool. Instead students are synthesizing their intentions in a brief and concise manner, and artistically creating a representation of what they want to learn and accomplish by visually setting SMART (specific, measurable, attainable, relevant, time-bound) goal(s).
- **Critical Thinking:** To synthesize their intentions in a brief and concise manner, students must spend quite a bit of time thinking critically about each aspect of the SMART goal. Also, when displaying the vision boards on the class website, students are asked to explain the reason(s) behind their choices. This allows their thinking to be visible to others.
- **Communication:** The whole goal of the assignment is for the students to communicate their ideas for others. Posting them in the classroom, hallway, or a website adds a variety of audiences to this assignment. *(Separating these three Cs in this assignment is almost impossible because they are woven together so closely.)*

Learning Outcomes

- Students will develop their ability to write a SMART goal.
- Students will synthesize what they really want to accomplish in a brief, concise, and visual way and share it with others to encourage a sense of accountability.
- Students will reflect on their learning and see how much they have learned over an 18-week period.

> **About Vicki Heupel**
>
> Vicki Heupel (hi-pull) is a high school science teacher in Bigfork, Montana. She teaches biology, forensics, and astronomy. Vicki is passionate about giving students more opportunities to engage in the doing of science—more experiments, more building, and more hands-on learning. Vicki is also a Google Certified Educator Level 1 and was featured in episode 26 of *The Shake Up Learning Show.*

Fake Instagram by Carly Black

Shakeup.link/fake
Grade Levels: 6–12
Subjects: Applicable in any content area
Google Tool: Google Slides
Dynamic Learning Characteristics

☑ Beyond the Bell
☑ Beyond the Subject or Grade Level
☑ Beyond the Tools
☑ Beyond the Walls
☐ Beyond the Due Date

Summary: Inspired by episode 32 of the *Shake Up Learning Show* podcast with Lisa Johnson, Carly took Lisa's fake Instagram template originally created in Apple Keynote and created a Google Slides version that she used with her own high school students. In this lesson, Students create an Instagram account using a fake Instagram template in Google Slides to depict relationships and important events within a narrative story. The fake Instagram template can easily be adapted for other content area activities.

ISTE Standards

- Students leverage technology to take an active role in choosing, achieving, and demonstrating competency in their learning goals, informed by the learning sciences.
- Students recognize the rights, responsibilities, and opportunities of living, learning, and working in an interconnected digital world, and they act and model in ways that are safe, legal, and ethical.
- Students critically curate a variety of resources, using digital tools to construct knowledge, produce creative artifacts, and make meaningful learning experiences for themselves and others.
- Students communicate clearly and express themselves creatively for a variety of purposes, using the platforms, tools, styles, formats, and digital media appropriate to their goals.

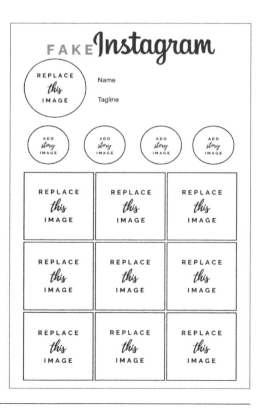

4 Cs

- **Critical Thinking**: Analyze how parts of a whole interact with each other to produce overall outcomes in complex texts.
- **Communication**: Effectively articulate the connections, significant factors, and new knowledge gained while reading through the use of images and modern language such as hashtags.
- **Creativity**: Demonstrate originality and inventiveness to visually represent understanding and analysis.

Learning Outcomes

- Students will be able to demonstrate their knowledge of how events impact people and characters.
- They will also demonstrate the skills of summarizing and drawing conclusions.

> **About Carly Black**
>
> Carly Black spends her days encouraging her middle school students to believe reading and writing is totally cool. At night she chases her tiny humans with her teacher husband, and in the morning repeats the process all over again. Find the lessons and ideas she uses to encourage her students and tame her tiny humans on the blog TeachMomRepeat.com.

#InnovatingPlay by Christine Pinto and Jessica Twomey

Shakeup.link/innplay
Grade Levels: K–2
Subjects: Applicable in any content area
Google Tool: Google Slides
Dynamic Learning Characteristics

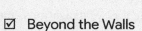

- ☑ Beyond the Bell
- ☐ Beyond the Subject or Grade Level
- ☑ Beyond the Tools
- ☑ Beyond the Walls
- ☐ Beyond the Due Date

Summary: This Dynamic Learning experience was created by Kindergarten teachers Christine Pinto and Jessica Twomey, co-authors of the book, *Innovating Play*. Innovating Play also happens to be the title of this learning experience, which allows children to explore diverse environments from a variety of perspectives. This adventure is a culminating activity for students to make connections between the city and the country using the five senses. Our connecting text was *City Kid, Country Kid* by Julie Cummins.

Students develop writing skills and descriptive vocabulary through use of their five senses. Their final product is a set of written and illustrated postcards communicating their

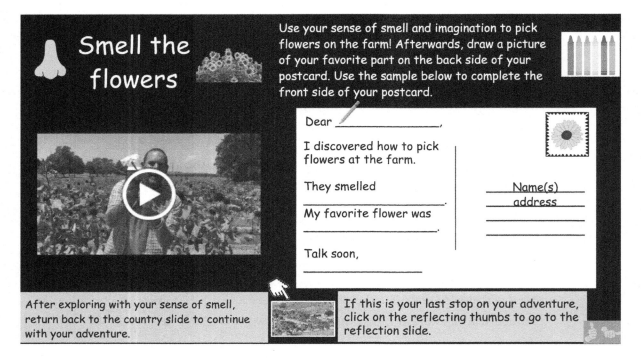

observations and discoveries. Students also participate in a choice menu of hands-on extension experiences.

ISTE Standards

- Students communicate complex ideas clearly and effectively by creating or using a variety of digital objects such as visualizations, models, or simulations.

4 Cs

Communication:

- Students articulate thoughts and ideas effectively using oral, written, and nonverbal communication skills in a variety of forms and contexts.
- Students learn to listen effectively to decipher meaning, including knowledge, values, attitudes, and intentions.

About Christine Pinto and Jessica Twomey

Christine Pinto and Jessica Twomey have been in the field of Early Childhood Education for more than eighteen years collectively. Their kindergarten classes have collaborated on a daily basis from their locations in California and New Jersey for a number of years. Christine and Jessica moderated the #InnovatingPlay/#GAfE4Littles Slow Flip Chat via Flipgrid for a year and a half, and are proud to be authors of the book *Innovating Play: Reimagining Learning through Meaningful Tech Integration*. When opportunities arise, Christine and Jessica travel to present about *Innovating Play* and how they preserve, protect, and transform early childhood experiences in and beyond the classroom. For more, check out their website: innovatingplay.world.

- Students use communication for a range of purposes (*e.g.*, to inform, instruct, motivate, and persuade).

Learning Outcomes

- Students will be able to share information about how people use their five senses to explore and discover about the world.
- Students will be able to draw and write to share information about places in the city or the country.
- Students will be able to tell the order of events and share their ideas.

Student Portfolios with Google Sites by Mike Mohammad

Shakeup.link/eport
Grade Levels: 6–12
Subjects: Applicable in any content area
Google Tools: Google Sites and various other Google tools throughout the year

Dynamic Learning Characteristics

☑ Beyond the Bell
☑ Beyond the Grade Level & Subject
☑ Beyond the Tools
☑ Beyond the Walls
☑ Beyond the Due Date

Summary: In this yearlong project by high school physics teacher Mike Mohammad, students create and update their own learning portfolios in Google Sites. Students build a digital portfolio using Google Sites over the length of the class or school year. The portfolio consists of pages that curate artifacts from the class to demonstrate learning outcomes. In addition, the portfolio describes the student as a learner and their interests in and out of the classroom. This portfolio is created at the start of the course, and students add to it at the end of every unit of instruction. Mike has been doing this for several years now, and his students show growth and creativity over time.

ISTE Standards

- Students articulate and set personal learning goals, develop strategies leveraging technology to achieve them, and reflect on the learning process itself to improve learning outcomes.
- Students cultivate and manage their digital identity and reputation and are aware of the permanence of their actions in the digital world.

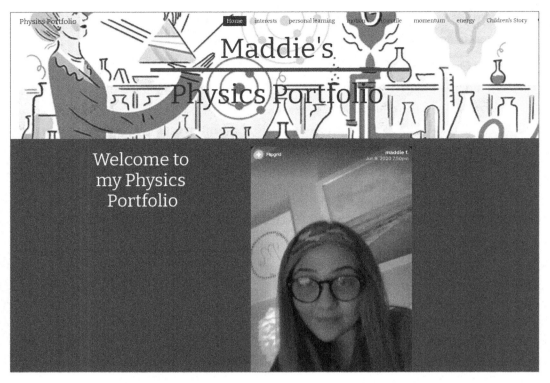

- Students choose the appropriate platforms and tools for meeting the desired objectives of their creation or communication.
- Students publish or present content that customizes the message and medium for their intended audiences.

4 Cs

- **Communication**: Effectively and clearly communicate for a variety of audiences and using a variety of tools and mediums
- **Critical Thinking**: Analyzing, synthesizing, and going deeper into meaning and content

Learning Outcomes

- Students will be able to present and defend evidence of learning from within a unit as it relates to learning outcomes.
- Students will be able to identify and communicate their strengths as a learner.

About Mike Mohammad

Mike Mohammad has been teaching high school science in Wisconsin for more than twenty years. Mike attended UW Madison, where he received his degree in Secondary Education in Broadfield Science and Biology with additional certifications in chemistry and physics. In his time at Brookfield Central, Mike has taught biology, chemistry, physics, and general science. His interests in education focus on putting students at the center of their own learning experience.

Your Community in 360 Degrees by Jessica Brogley

Shakeup.link/360
Grade Levels: 3–5 (can also be adapted for 6-12)
Subjects: Language Arts and Social Studies
Google Tools: Google Maps

Dynamic Learning Characteristics

☐ Beyond the Bell
☑ Beyond the Subject or Grade Level
☑ Beyond the Tools
☑ Beyond the Walls
☑ Beyond the Due Date

Summary: In this learning experience by Geo expert Jessica Brogley, students learn how to use 360-degree cameras to document, create, and learn about their local community. Students will place those 360-degree images on Google Maps as "photospheres." Students will make local connections with partners and create a product that benefits their entire community.

ISTE Standards

- Students leverage technology to take an active role in choosing, achieving, and demonstrating competency in their learning goals, informed by the learning sciences.
- Students recognize the rights, responsibilities, and opportunities of living, learning, and working in an interconnected digital world, and they act and model in ways that are safe, legal, and ethical.

Learning Outcomes

- Students will learn about essential services and attractions in their local community.
- Students will learn how to photograph these locations and attractions from every angle.

4 Cs

- **Creativity:** Students learn the art and technical skills of using 360-degree photography to tell a story.
- **Collaboration:** Students work together with local partners to create a meaningful story for the community.

About Jessica Brogley

Jessica Brogley has over twenty years of experience in public schools teaching English Language Arts, supporting technology integration, and facilitating school communications. Currently, she teaches courses in educational technology in the School of Education at the University of Wisconsin-Platteville and is the host of the Proud Rural Teacher Podcast. Jessica is also a Google for Education Certified Trainer and Innovator. Additionally, she is a leader with the Global Google Educator Group and the founder of the Southwest Wisconsin Google Educator Group. To boot, she's also Google Streetview Certified and is a Level 8 Google Local Guide where she's committed to using Google Maps and Earth to tell the digital story of Southwest Wisconsin.

Blogging, Vlogging, and Podcasting in Google Classroom by Laura Steinbrink

Shakeup.link/vlog
Grade Levels: 4–12
Subjects: Applicable in any content area
Google Tools: Google Classroom, Google Sites, and Google Forms

Dynamic Learning Characteristics

- ☑ Beyond the Bell
- ☐ Beyond the Subject or Grade Level
- ☑ Beyond the Tools
- ☐ Beyond the Walls
- ☐ Beyond the Due Date

Summary: In this learning experience designed for upper elementary through high school–aged students, Laura Steinbrink, high school teacher and district technology coach, uses Google Classroom as the hub for her students to have a safe controlled platform for receiving feedback on their blogs, vlogs, or podcasts, as well as an authentic audience for their stories, thoughts, and opinions. Students learn how to give specific feedback on top of the written and oral communication practice.

Laura starts by setting up a special Google Classroom Class designated for blogging and adds all her students. She then creates a topic and assignment named for each student inside Google Classroom. Students submit the links to their blogs as a comment to make them viewable by all class members. Students comment on each other's blogs to help each other grow as writers. Laura requires her students to read the posts of three other students weekly and comment with specific feedback for the student author.

Alexis T.				
Tyler P.	**Kelsey T.**			⋮
Kevan M.	? Kelsey T.		Edited 9:46 PM	
Case M.	No due date			
Jacob M.	To comment on her blog, click the link below. Remember to put the blog post title in your comment so that she knows the one to which you are referring.		0	1
Cecilia G.			Turned in	Assigned
Katelyn F.	Katelyn's Blog https://spark.adobe.com/pag…			
Damon C.				
Dominic B.	View Question			

ISTE Standards

- Students use technology to seek feedback that informs and improves their practice and to demonstrate their learning in a variety of ways.
- Students engage in positive, safe, legal, and ethical behavior when using technology, including social interactions online or when using networked devices.
- Students choose the appropriate platforms and tools for meeting the desired objectives of their creation or communication.
- Students publish or present content that customizes the message and medium for their intended audiences.
- Students create original works or responsibly repurpose or remix digital resources into new creations.

4 Cs

- **Communication**: Synthesize and share ideas in both written and oral forms
- **Creativity**: Learn how to see what's not there and make something happen
- **Critical Thinking**: Make decisions, solve problems, and take action

Learning Outcomes

- Students can review, revise, and edit writing with consideration for the task, purpose, and audience.
- Students will be able to organize content-introduce the topic, maintain clear focus throughout the text, and provide a conclusion that follows from the text.
- Achieve the writer's purpose and demonstrate an awareness of audience by making choices regarding organization and content.
- Students will be able to use technology, including the internet, to produce, publish, and update individual or shared writing products, taking advantage of technology's capacity to link to other information and to display information flexibly and dynamically.
- Students can follow a writing process focusing on development, organization, style, and voice to produce clear and coherent writing.

> **About Laura Steinbrink**
>
> Laura Steinbrink, a teacher for twenty-five years, presents technology and instructional practices at workshops locally, around her state, and nationally. She is also an education consultant, technology integration coach, communications director, webmaster, yearbook adviser, esports general manager, and high school English/Spanish teacher for the Plato R-V School District in Missouri. Laura is the author of rockntheboat.com.

Shapegrams by Tony Vincent

Shakeup.link/shapegrams
Grade Levels: 3–9
Subjects: Art, Science, and Math
Google Tools: Google Classroom, Google Sites, and Google Forms

Dynamic Learning Characteristics

☑ Beyond the Bell   ☐ Beyond the Walls
☐ Beyond the Subject or Grade Level   ☑ Beyond the Due Date
☑ Beyond the Tools

Summary: Tony Vincent is one of the most creative educators I know. I've admired his work for many years. Tony has created a program called Shapegrams (Shapegrams.com). Shapegrams are digital drawing challenges in which students not only learn digital drawing skills but are also challenged to think critically to recreate the drawing challenge. Each Shapegram is a Google Drawings document that contains a picture to recreate, an instructional video, design tips, and extension activities. Students practice visual observation skills and critical thinking as they learn drawing tools and techniques. Each Shapegram in

the sequence builds on the skills learned in the previous Shapegram. There are thirty-six challenges, but even after completing the first four, students will have skills to create their own illustrations. If a student completes all thirty-six challenges, they will be able to create illustrations, diagrams, models, and just about anything else they might want to draw.

ISTE Standards

- Students use a variety of technologies within a design process to identify and solve problems by creating new, useful, or imaginative solutions.
- Students create original works or responsibly repurpose or remix digital resources into new creations.
- Students communicate complex ideas clearly and effectively by creating or using a variety of digital objects such as visualizations, models, or simulations.

4 Cs

- **Communication**: Effectively and clearly communicate for a variety of audiences and using a variety of tools and mediums
- **Critical Thinking**: Analyzing, synthesizing, and going deeper into meaning and content
- **Creativity**: Use of imagination and original ideas to solve problems and create

Learning Outcomes

- Students will be able to examine a picture and recreate it using shapes and lines.
- Students will be able to apply their drawing skills to craft their own illustrations, icons, diagrams, and models.

> #### *About Tony Vincent*
> After years of self-employment as an education and technology presenter, Tony went back to the classroom to teach fifth grade in Council Bluffs, Iowa, for the 2018–2019 school year. Although he's proud to have led workshops and presentations in almost all fifty states, empowering his students to be creative communicators is his favorite professional accomplishment. An edtech pioneer since 1998, Tony creates and shares resources for teachers through his blog, LearninginHand.com.

The Dynamic Learning Experience Database

In *Shake Up Learning*, I introduced a searchable lesson plan database, The Dynamic Learning Experience database. This database includes lessons from my books and lessons from teachers like you, and it is where you can find ideas and share your own.

ShakeUpLearning.link/DLdatabase

OUR DYNAMIC LEARNING PLAN

Now that you have made it through all of the chapters and reviewed the lesson plan examples, it's your turn to plan a Dynamic Learning experience for your classroom!

Let's review the planning cycle from the Dynamic Learning Model.

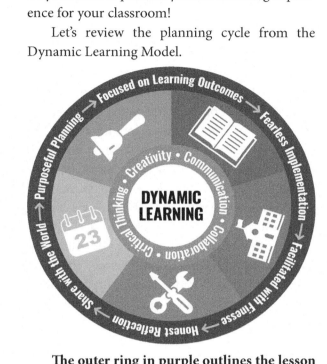

The outer ring in purple outlines the lesson planning cycle:

- **Purposeful Planning**—Planning for meaningful learning takes time and thought. By throwing things together last-minute, you risk losing focus and wasting valuable instructional time.
- **Focused on Learning Outcomes**—Begin with the end in mind! Backwards design will help ensure that you plan learning experiences that will directly correlate with your learning goals and standards.
- **Fearless Implementation**—Meaningful change and growth requires risk-taking. Get comfortable with being

uncomfortable. You will never know what you and your students are capable of without stepping outside your comfort zone.

- **Facilitated with Finesse**—Lesson planning doesn't end with a good plan. The plan must include good facilitation strategies. How will you guide your students? How will you support their learning path?
- **Honest Reflection**—Reflection is critical to the learning process and to improve your craft as a teacher. Make time to honestly reflect on your lessons. What went well? What do you need to improve?
- **Share with the World**—There is so much that educators can learn from one another if you are just willing to share. That's why I have created the lesson plan database. Share your lessons so that other teachers can adapt and grow in their own classrooms.

Planning Questions and Tips

Before you jump into the lesson plan template, take some time to brainstorm on the ideas shared in this book, review your notes, and think about where you are in your own classroom. Make sure to consider and plan for the following:

- **Learning Targets**—What are the big ideas we want learners to understand and use? What unit of study are you currently planning or will be planning soon? What are your learning goals?
- **Essential Questions**—What provocative questions will foster inquiry, understanding, and transfer of learning?

- **Assessment Evidence**—How will we know learners have understood the big ideas? How will you know they "get it"?
- **Learning Experiences and Instruction**—What learning activities will facilitate understanding of the big ideas? Will this learning take place in a face-to-face classroom, remotely, or a hybrid? How will you engage students given the learning environment?
- **Technology Tools**—How will technology (and Google tools) enhance and support the learning?
- **Dynamic Learning Goals**—How can you step out of your comfort zone and take risks? How will this lesson extend beyond a normal one-and-done activity? What opportunities will learners have to continue the learning? How will learners communicate, collaborate, and extend the learning?

Facilitation and Technology Tips

Dynamic Blended Learning requires that the teacher take on the role of facilitator, which is easier said than done. Some of these are just good reminders from what we've covered in previous chapters. Below are some of my best facilitation and technology tips.

Shift Your Mindset

I hear from people all the time who say, "I'm just not good with technology." Make up your mind to be positive. Mindset is the biggest battle to overcoming technology fears! The classroom is full of obstacles; technology is no different. Maybe you aren't as quick to learn with technology as

your peers, but never let that become an excuse. If your mind is holding you back, you have some internal work to do. Take the time to reflect on your current mindset and approach technology with a positive and flexible attitude.

Take Risks

The magic happens outside of your comfort zone. Don't be afraid to step out and try new things in the classroom. Model risk-taking in your classroom. Let your students know when you fail or make a mistake so that they understand that is okay. Find ways to push students out of their comfort zones, give them new ideas, perspectives, and ways to approach a problem that can help them see the value in failing forward. Taking a risk during the learning process is a gamble, but one that can pay off big time. The difference is that a risk in the classroom may not guarantee success, but if truly guided with purpose toward the learning goals can garner valuable learning along the way.

Start with the Why

When you are planning a digital learning experience, be goal oriented! Begin with your learning outcomes, not the technology. This idea is perhaps the most important tip of all. Everything we do as teachers should always come down student learning and doing what's best for kids. Just because you are using technology doesn't ensure you are meeting any objectives or learning outcomes. If you cannot explain how the digital tool enhances or improves the learning experience, you are just using technology for technology's sake. If this is the case, start over!

I can't tell you how many conversations I've had with teachers that have started with this question, "How can I use [insert digital tool name] in my classroom?" The question should never be how to "fit" this awesome new tool into your learning experience. The question is always, "What are the desired student outcomes? What do you want them to understand and be able to do?" Then you find the best tools in your toolbox to help you get there.

Be Consistent

When technology changes so fast, and new digital tools become available every minute, it can be tempting to try something new in your classroom every day, but learners need consistency. We all know how frustrating it can be to try something new that requires additional set-up time and then doesn't really do everything you had hoped. Balance tried and true tools with sprinkles of new stuff to keep it interesting. You don't want to be so consistent that it becomes predictable and mundane.

Don't Integrate Too Many Tools At Once

Start small. Along with being consistent, resist the urge to integrate too many digital tools at once. If you try to do too much at once, you risk shifting the focus to the tool and just using technology for technology's sake. If you love tech like I do, it can be easy to keep adding more ideas and tools to your lesson. But you should gradually build your student's digital toolbox. It doesn't have to happen in one day!

Don't Be Afraid to Let Your Students Teach You!

Our students have a lot of knowledge and skills, especially when it comes to technology. Long gone are the days of the teacher being the gatekeepers of knowledge. It's okay if you don't know the answer when it comes to the technology,

and students will love the chance to help teach you! As you are designing your learning experience, and you wonder about how a digital tool works or if there an app for that, ask a student! And even if they do not know the answer, they will be willing to help you figure it out!

Utilize Student Tech Experts

It's a myth to assume that every student is comfortable with technology. We still have a huge digital divide. But there are experts among us in our classrooms that can help bridge that gap. So not only should you leverage students to help you learn new digital skills, but you should also use them as go-to experts for other students in your classroom. This kind of leadership can be a very empowering experience for students. It can also help those with inclinations toward technology to explore their passions and interests, and it can definitely help get more girls and young women interested in technology as well.

Ask Three Before Me

In my classroom, I would often deliver small group instruction while the rest of the class worked on other assignments, stations or learning menus. It became difficult to manage questions while I was working with my small group. Some learners just naturally go to the teacher with every little problem, and often times, these questions are easily answered by other learners in the classroom or found online. By implementing the, "ask three before me," strategy my learners helped each other problem solve and complete their tasks and assignments, while I focused on my small group. This, of course, works well when digital tools are involved. If a student forgets how to log in, or where the rubric is saved, they can easily ask another student instead of interrupting the teacher.

> **Pro Tip:** You can also make YouTube and Google Search one of the three options to ask for help.

Get Organized

One of the best things you can do as a facilitator of digital learning is to organize the information, directions, objectives, and resources online for your learners. Consider using Google Classroom or Google Sites as your classroom hub. Giving learners *one* central location or website will make your life easier and will allow learners to focus on the learning tasks. It also helps you keep the learning experience as paperless as possible!

Package Your Online Assignments

Don't miss out on one of the best things about managing assignments online! When you create an assignment online using Google Classroom (or other preferred tool), give learners all of the information online. Give them detailed directions, the rubric, the due date, detail collaborative expectations, where and how to turn it in, what to do if they finish early, *everything* you can think of! This will save you time answering questions.

It is also convenient for absent work and demanding parents. This can also serve as documentation, a record of your lesson plans. You can fine tune things and revise as you see fit throughout the assignment.

Don't Assess the Bells and Whistles; Content is King

Technology can bring some excitement and engagement to student products and projects. But when it comes to assessing student work, always remember to go back to those learning goals. What was the original purpose of the lesson? Was it to include three animations in a PowerPoint? I hope not! The fun little extras, the bells, and whistles can give something special to a project, but that is most likely not your end goal.

Steer clear of rubrics that rely strictly on numbers, like the number of slides, the number of pictures, etc. Instead, use a rubric that focuses on the content and skills that the lesson was designed to teach.

Always Have a Plan B

No matter how much you prepare for any lesson—even the ones that don't involve technology—things do not always go as planned. We have all experienced those times when the technology doesn't cooperate: the internet connection or Wi-Fi is down, the website you were using crashed, the video you were going to play is blocked, the digital tool you planned to use is no longer free. It happens to all of us! That is why it is crucial to not only think on your feet but to also have a Plan B. Plan B doesn't mean a completely new lesson plan, but it does mean knowing what you will do if the lesson just isn't working out. Sometimes this means going back to pen and paper. Sometimes this means going back to a tried and true tool like Google Docs. Being flexible is nothing new if you are a teacher, integrating technology is no different. Be prepared to transition to Plan B before you lose an entire instructional period.

LESSON PLAN TEMPLATE
(DYNAMIC BLENDED LEARNING EXPERIENCE TEMPLATE)

I have created a lesson plan template, better known as the Dynamic Blended Learning Experience template, that you can use to plan your lesson using the Dynamic Learning Framework.

Because I want this book to be truly effective, the challenge in this chapter is perhaps the greatest. It's time to step into action. Below is the Dynamic Blended Learning Experience planning template that will help you plan your learning experience.

You can make a copy of the Google Doc lesson plan template by going here: shakeup.link/DLEtemplate.

One-Page Template

I have also created a simplified, one-page template for those that find the planning process overwhelming or for those who are well-versed in purposeful planning.

The Power of Reflection for Teachers

Reflection is a critical part of the learning process for students and for teachers to improve their craft. Take the time to reflect on what went well, what didn't, and how you could adapt it for remote learning if necessary.

- What lessons went well?
- What lessons bombed?
- What went well during remote learning? What didn't?
- What did you learn about your students?
- How did you engage students?
- How did you communicate with students and families?
- How can you improve?

If we don't take time to reflect, we risk repeating mistakes. Let's make sure we improve as we move forward.

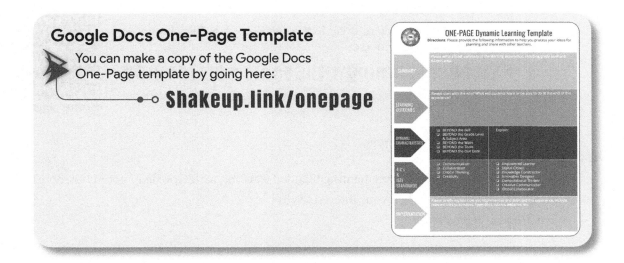

Google Docs One-Page Template

You can make a copy of the Google Docs One-Page template by going here:

Shakeup.link/onepage

Share with the World!

I also want to encourage you to complete that last step in the cycle, share with the world! Please, take advantage of my dynamic learning database of lessons! Explore it and share your lessons to help other teachers.

Every teacher has something unique to share! Don't underestimate the impact you could have just by sharing your lessons and ideas.

ShakeUpLearning.link/DLdatabase

Online Resources for Chapter 8

Here you will find resources mentioned in Chapter 8, supplemental resources, videos, as well as new and updated resources.

BlendedLearningwithGoogle.com/8

Online Course: Module 8

Dig deeper and get hands-on tutorials in the online course. This chapter aligns with Module 8 in the course.

BlendedLearningwithGoogle.com/course

Discussion Questions

- What ideas do you have for implementing blended learning with Google in your classroom?
- Which sample lessons sparked your interest? Why?
- What are your next steps?

Notes & Reflection Space

I pursued Google Certification and became a Google Certified Trainer in 2014. That decision changed my thinking, my career, and gave me the skills to teach and learn online. I am also a Google Certified Educator Level 1 and Level 2, and a Google Certified Innovator. You can hear more about my Google Certification story in

Episode 39 of *The Shake Up Learning Show*.

I don't work for Google. They don't pay me to share Google tips and strategies. I share them because these free, easy-to-use tools are readily accessible from any device. Most of all, I share Google tools and tactics because I know they can empower educators to make learning dynamic—be it in onsite, online, or hybrid classrooms.

Building capacity and increasing your Google skills is more important than ever. The Google Certification program is more than just a badge or certificate. It's a journey, a process. You don't have to be certified to learn with and share Google tools, but speaking from experience, becoming Google Certified is one of the best learning decisions I've made to date.

What is the Google Certification Program?

Google offers five certifications specifically for educators, Google Certified Educator Level 1, Google Certified Educator Level 2, Google Certified Trainer, Google Certified Innovator, and Google Certified Coach. The Certified Educator program is designed to help teachers learn how to use Google tools through blended learning models. Google Certified Trainers, Innovators, and Coaches are leadership programs for those ready to lead professional development and change in their schools.

Google Certified Educator Level 1 and Level 2

The Google Certified Educator program was designed for the classroom teacher but is open for any educator to pursue.

The Certified Educator program is offered at two levels: the fundamentals level (Level 1), and the advanced level (Level 2). Differentiating the certification into two levels gives more teachers an opportunity to get recognized for the work they've done.

Below are just a few of the benefits of the Google Certified Educator program.

Level 1

Level 1 Google Certified Educator status indicates that an educator is able to successfully implement Google for Education into their teaching practice to enhance teaching and learning.

This certification is for educators with a basic understanding of the core features of Google for Education as well as well as an understanding of how to meaningfully use technology in the classroom.

Shakeuplearning.com/level1resources

Level 2

Level 2 Google Certified Educator status indicates that an educator is able to integrate a wider range of Google for Education tools and other technologies to transform their teaching practice.

This is for educators with a deeper understanding of Google for Education and advanced technology integration skills.

Shakeuplearning.com/level2resources

Gain Confidence with Digital Learning Strategies and Google Tools

You don't know what you don't know! And there is always something new to learn about Google tools! Even if you are an experienced Google apps user, you will learn something new, including new ways to use Google tools in the classroom. The more you know and use these tools, the more confident you will be in your own classroom and teaching others.

No one has ever come out of my Level 1 training and said, "I knew all that," and if they did, they'd be fibbing at least a little. We can't know it all and retain it all at once.

The more we know and understand Google for Education, cloud computing, and using Google tools for learning, the more confidence we will have to use them and try new applications and strategies. Confidence cannot be undersold! This makes all the difference in the world when it comes to technology integration and remote learning. Even teachers that I know have had the skills for years don't have confidence. Proving their skills through the certification program changed everything.

Facilitate and Inspire Student Learning and Creativity

The Google Certified Educator program isn't just about the technology; it is learning how to use these tools to facilitate meaningful learning experiences for your students. (Now, doesn't that fit so nicely with the ideas in this book!) Through this program, you will learn how to use Google tools to support and deepen learning in your classroom, create meaningful assessments, give feedback, as well as ideas for inspiring creativity in your students.

Create a Paperless Classroom

Google tools can help you learn how to create a paperless classroom and improve your digital workflow and grading. Creating a paperless classroom is usually one of the first steps for educators using Google tools, but after you learn how to go beyond just substitution, you can use Google to create Dynamic Blended Learning experiences for your students. One thing is certainly clear. Those who have clung to old-school static lessons, and then tried to replicate them in a digital environment, did not engage their students. It's not about taking our old ways and putting them online in Google Classroom; it's about rethinking our assignments.

Collect Data and Increase Feedback Loops

Assessment data is a critical part of any classroom! Using Google Forms and Google Sheets, you will learn how to collect all kinds of data from your students and improve feedback.

During remote learning, traditional grading strategies are much more difficult. Suddenly, timely feedback was at the forefront, as it should have been all along. Teachers can learn how to use Google tools to improve feedback and collect data beyond a traditional test.

Learn How to Find Answers and Support

What do you do when you get stuck? Do you know who to ask for support? Do you know where to search? When you have questions, it's important to understand how to search the support center, help forums, and find assistance when you need it.

Yikes! Who needs this now more than ever? By the way, bookmark support.google.com now. This link is your new best friend! But through the certification process, teachers also learn about many other places to connect and find support.

Increase Digital Citizenship and Digital Literacy Skills in the Classroom

Finding time to teach digital citizenship skills can sometimes feel impossible. Google offers many ways to support these skills and help you find practical moments to build this skill set with your students.

Can I get an amen? I mean, seriously, y'all! Have we ever seen more need for digital literacy and citizenship skills? Learning how to behave online, in video chats, in online discussions, and what to do if something goes wrong—there's never been a more opportune moment!

Increase Efficiency and Save Time

Through the certification program, educators learn how to use Google tools to save time and become more efficient. The number one complaint of most teachers is lack of time. What if technology could actually save you time? When you learn how to use digital tools to be a more efficient teacher, everyone wins!

I always say that time-saving tips are the best buy-in for teachers who struggle with technology. Google tools should make working and teaching easier, not more complicated, but good professional development makes the difference. If teachers are not given the opportunity to learn in a meaningful way, differentiated for their skill level, they will always struggle.

Engage in Professional Growth and Leadership

Are you a lifelong learner? You should be! That's part of a growth mindset (Beyond the Bell) and will help you learn and grow with your students. Teachers have always had to be flexible, but these days they are stretched to the limits. There has never been more opportunity to stretch the mindset and build capacity and leadership.

Prove Your Skills

Teachers have to learn so much; isn't it nice when you are recognized for your accomplishments? When you become a Google Certified Educator, you get a certificate and badge that proves you know your stuff! Don't underestimate the power of recognition. We all need validation.

Get the Badge and Join the Google Certified Family

Share your badge in your email signature, your blog, or your website, and wear it proud. Google Certified Educators are part of an elite group, a family of teachers that share and grow together.

Google Certified Trainer

The Google for Education Certified Trainer program is designed for educators with a strong history of providing Google training in schools, including creating informative learning materials and sharing enthusiasm for digital learning and technology.

Trainer Resources

If you are in a position where you deliver Google training to other educators, or desire a training position, this program can take your career to the next level.

 **Shakeuplearning.com/trainerresources**

Google Certified Innovator

The Google for Education Certified Innovator Program supports educators in developing new projects for their classrooms and school districts. Members participate in a year-long mentorship program that begins with workshops called Innovator Academies, where teachers, coaches, and Google experts learn from each other.

The Certified Innovator program is the most competitive of them all. Only a select few are accepted into the program each year. This elite group is made up of educational leaders and change-makers!

Google Certified Coach

The Google Certified Coach program empowers instructional coaches to work 1:1 with educators and drive impactful technology use in their schools. Coaches get access to research-backed strategies and tools so that new and veteran educators alike can transform instruction across every classroom.

SHAKE UP LEARNING GOOGLE CERTIFICATION ACADEMIES

Shake Up Learning offers online, self-paced courses to help you reach your Google Certification goals:

- The Google Certified Educator Level 1 Academy
- The Google Certified Educator Level 2 Academy
- The Google Certified Trainer Academy
- More academies coming soon!

Get Google Certified

Learn more about Google Certifications:

GetGoogleCertified.com

Google Training for Schools

Do you need help getting your entire team, campus, or school district Google Certified and up-to-speed with Google tools? We also offer deep discounts for large groups on our online courses and books.

GoogleTrainingforSchools.com

Online Resources for Chapter 9

 Here you will find resources mentioned in Chapter 9, supplemental resources, videos, as well as new and updated resources.

BlendedLearningwithGoogle.com/9

Online Course: Module 9

Dig deeper and get hands-on tutorials in the online course. This chapter aligns with Module 9 in the course.

BlendedLearningwithGoogle.com/course

Discussion Questions

- Is Google Certification right for you? What's holding you back?
- Challenge: share your Google Certification goals on social with the #shakeuplearning hashtag!

Notes & Reflection Space

closing

efore I skedaddle, let me take a moment to thank you for coming along on this journey with me. Being a teacher is one of the toughest jobs! I hope the ideas shared in this book will help you grow as an educator, push your skills further, and most of all, I hope this book helps your students.

We've covered a lot of ground in this book—from guiding principles to implementation. Don't let it overwhelm you. Take it one step at a time. No teacher is perfect. Always accept the challenges before you as an opportunity to do what's best for kids.

I challenge you to . . .

- be a dynamic learning facilitator
- ignite the ordinary,
- be an UNCOMMON educator,
- teach with audaciousness,
- be bold,
- and to have audacious faith in your students.
- Now go ...**SHAKE UP LEARNING!**

BYE, Y'ALL!

Which Book Should I Read Next?

The Shake Up Learning Book Series

Google from A–Z: The Google Glossary for Teachers—If you haven't picked up this supplement and reference guide to all things Google, grab a copy and keep it handy as you use Google tools throughout the year.

Shake Up Learning: Practical Ideas to Move Learning from Static to Dynamic—The first book in the Shake Up Learning series takes a deep dive into the Dynamic Learning Framework, the why, the what, and the how!

Look for more Shake Up Learning books coming soon!
→ **ShakeUpLearningBooks.com**

Bibliography

Collaborative for Academic, Social, and Emotional Learning. CASEL.org. Accessed October 18, 2020. Casel.org

Forleo, M. *Everything Is Figureoutable*. New York: Penguin; 2019.

Locke, E. A., Latham, G. P. (2006). New Directions in Goal-Setting Theory. *Current Directions in Psychological Science*, 15⑤, 265-268.

Matthews, G. (2015). Goal Research Summary. Paper presented at the 9th Annual International Conference of the Psychology Research Unit of Athens Institute for Education and Research (ATINER), Athens, Greece.

HyperDocs." https://hyperdocs.co. Accessed 21 Sep. 2020.

What is PBL? (2020). Accessed October 11, 2020. https://www.pblworks.org/what-is-pbl

Acknowledgments

A special thank you to all of the educators who contributed to this book.

Lisa Johnson

Mike Mohammad

Pam Hubler

Vicki Heupel

Tony Vincent

Christine Pinto

Jessica Twomey

Jessica Brogley

Sylvia Duckworth

Laura Steinbrink

Tommy Spall

GOOGLE RESOURCES

Google Resources from ShakeUpLearning.com

The award-winning Shake Up Learning website and blog provides teachers with practical resources for using technology in the classroom. You'll find tips and strategies on how to use Google Classroom, Google for Education, and other Google tools. In addition, ShakeUpLearning.com offers many other blended learning and technology integration resources.

Find technology tips and tricks, free downloads and templates, in-depth online courses, books, lesson plans, lesson ideas, cheat sheets, blog publications, and podcasts.

Access free Google resources, tips, and downloads
→ ShakeUpLearning.com/google

Free Google Classroom Resources
→ ShakeUpLearning.com/googleclassroom

Subscribe and Get a Freebie
→ ShakeUpLearning.com/subscribe

Online Courses from Shake Up Learning

Shake Up Learning offers a variety of online, self-paced courses on many Google topics, including Google Classroom, Google Slides, and Google Certification. We also offer online workshops on dynamic learning and meaningful technology integration.

Some of our most popular courses include:

- The Google Classroom Master Class
- The Google Slides Master Class
- The Google Certification Academies
- The Dynamic Learning Workshop

Join today to take your blended learning skills to the next level!

Shake Up Learning Online Courses

→ **ShakeUpLearning.com/courses**

Shake Up Learning offers free resources and webinars to help educators get Google Certified. Let Kasey be your guide on your journey to becoming a Google Certified Educator, Level 1, Level 2, or even become a Google Certified Trainer.

Get Google Certified

→ **GetGoogleCertified.com**

Need Google Training for Your Entire School?

Look no further! Shake Up Learning offers a variety of programs to help your teachers learn how to meaningfully integrate Google tools and the entire suite in the classroom. From online courses to books to face-to-face training, we've got you covered!

COVID-19 forced many teachers and schools to scramble to find tools to deliver online assignments and design digital learning experiences. Google was the number one suite of tools to help make this a reality!

Shake Up Learning empowers educators with just-in-time resources to keep learning relevant and meaningful—even during quarantine. When students return to school, Google skills will help set the foundation for more dynamic learning in the classroom.

Get your entire campus or district on board with Google! Help your teachers learn more about Google tools, Google Classroom, and meaningful technology integration strategies. You can even help your teachers become Google Certified Educators!

Learn More and Watch a Free Webinar
⟶ **GoogleTrainingForSchools.com**

Join the Community

Fans and readers of *Shake Up Learning* make up an extraordinary community of like-minded educators who are dedicated to making a difference in the lives of students. They wake up each day ready to shake up learning! As creator of *Shake Up Learning,* I wanted an online space where readers and fans could connect, find encouragement, share ideas, support one another, and discuss *Shake Up Learning* blog posts, resources, and this book.

I look forward to seeing you there!

Connect with the community
on social media using
#ShakeUpLearning

If you'd like to connect with me on
Twitter, Instagram, or TikTok, follow
@ShakeUpLearning

Join the Community!

Join the *Shake Up Learning* community of inspired educators. Here you can connect with others who are also practicing ideas to create dynamic, meaningful learning.

 **ShakeUpLearning.com/community**

with Kasey Bell

The Shake Up Learning Show is a weekly podcast hosted by Kasey Bell. The show, designed for K–12 teachers and educators, features tech tips, lesson ideas, practical advice, on-air coaching, student interviews, and interviews with inspiring educators.

New episodes are released every Tuesday. You can find The Shake Up Learning Show on Apple Podcasts, Google Podcasts, Stitcher, Spotify, or wherever you find your favorite podcasts. You can also stream on ShakeUpLearning.com.

The Shake Up Learning Show with Kasey Bell

→ **ShakeUpLearningShow.com**

Bring the Power of Kasey Bell and the Shake Up Learning Message to Your School, District, or Event!

With more than thirteen years' experience as a speaker, presenter, and professional learning facilitator, and over seventeen years' experience as an educator, Kasey Bell brings her unique brand of practical teaching ideas, inspiration, bold personality, and southern charm to every engagement. She has traveled the world delivering inspirational keynotes, workshops, and interactive conference presentations at world-renowned conferences, school districts, and private schools, and has even hosted her own events. Kasey has spoken at the International Society for Technology in Education (ISTE) Conference, Texas Computer Educators Association (TCEA) Convention, the Teach Tech Play Conference in Melbourne, Australia, Future of Education Technology Conference (FETC), Michigan Association for Computer Users in Learning (MACUL), and is regularly invited by Google to present to educators around the globe.

For more information, go to shakeuplearning.com/workwithme

What Teachers Are Saying about Kasey Bell ...

"Best session I went to at FETC. ... So much wonderful information and every bit of it useful!"
—Luanne Rowland

"I was very excited to hear someone present on ideas that are important to me. I teach special education and have been 'shaking up' the learning for my students for years. I have often been criticized for my approach, and at times reprimanded. It is past time that education takes on a new approach. Thank you for being a leader and voice for change."
—Candance Baty

"If you are attending a conference, follow these steps: 1. Search by presenter. 2. Find Kasey Bell. 3. Put all her sessions on your schedule! You will learn so much and have a great time doing it!"
—Stacy Menifee

"Kasey's trainings are ALWAYS worth it! This session was packed with ideas I could implement right away!"
—Laura Swearingen

"Kasey Bell was amazing. I appreciated her energy, expertise and experience. The examples, strategies, and resources she shared were so valuable and accessible for people at all levels. Thank you so much for the opportunity to hear her speak and learn from/with her. I could spend hours hearing her talk about her ideas."
—ERLC Innovation Summit in Edmonton, Canada, participant

"Loved your session! I attended two last time you attended KySTE. Your enthusiasm is amazing and definitely encourages us to be our better selves for our students."
—Autumn Mattingly

About the Author

Kasey Bell is part sparkling smile, part witty personality, and a whole heap of passion as big as Texas. As a former middle school teacher with nearly seventeen years in education, Kasey has made it her mission to be a disruptor of the boring and to push the bounds of traditional teaching and learning.

Kasey found her true passion in digital learning. With a master's degree in educational technology and a whole bunch of crazy ideas, she migrated to the role of instructional technologist. Now, Kasey is a digital learning coach, consultant, and trainer for Shake Up Learning, based in Texas. As her passion grew, so did her need to share and connect, and Kasey started sharing her passions through her blog, ShakeUpLearning.com.

Kasey is an engaging, innovative, from-the-heart sharer who inspires educators while transforming their teaching with original, dynamic, and use-tomorrow ideas for student choice, differentiation, and technology integration. Whether creating learning from home through online courses, leading conference workshops, or presenting as a keynote speaker, Kasey is a relentless innovator of ideas and a devoted transformer of classrooms and teaching.

Through the *Shake Up Learning Show* podcast, teacher-empowering books and workshops, and the award-winning educational resources offered at ShakeUpLearning.com, Kasey proves that educators should never settle for the static and boring. When it comes to bringing out the very best in our students, we should always strive to Shake Up Learning!

Made in the USA
Las Vegas, NV
30 January 2021